April. Caroline Roberts.

Grafik had the rather unfortunate experience of visiting the London Book Fair recently. Normally held at Olympia (which is no great shakes as a venue), this year the organisers saw fit to move it to the hell hole that is Excel, deep in the heart of what can only be described as the arse end of London. Grafik's not opposed to a bit of East-End grittiness but you have to admit that the area still has a very, very long way to go.

While Grafik knows that it's hard to find the space for a large conference centre in the middle of town, we don't mind a bit of a schlep if there's something good when you actually get there. Excel is the stuff of nightmares—it's so huge that there's room for several events to run at the same time, hence the rather strange combination of Book Fair delegates and visitors to Professional Beauty 2006. Those who find themselves in E16 and are in need of a cheap thrill this month should check out Salute, "an exhibition of playing games to recreate famous battles by way of war gaming, role-playing and military modeling", organised by the extremely scary-sounding South London Warlords.

Of course, whenever you create a one-size-fits-all environment, things are bound to err on the bland side, but after an hour in Excel you simply lose the will to live. The experience is a bit like being trapped in a huge, soulless, airless, out-of-town shopping mall—along with shuffling, blank-faced people, a 'continental' food hall, fantastically over-priced shops and the supremely naff Fox Bar and Diner.

The Book Fair itself was pretty much the same as ever. It's always nice to catch up with a few old friends, even if you do have to wade through acres of tat in the form of celebrity biographies and cute kitten calendars to do so. Unfortunately it took Grafik longer than usual due to the fact that we were too tight to fork out for the £20 showguide that contained the only portable map.

It was a truly horrible afternoon, only made bearable by one thing. While browsing on the Laurence King stand, Grafik came across the new offering from self-styled design critic Rick Poynor. On the back of his latest book was a quote lifted from none other than your favourite graphic design mag (albeit in an article by one of his mates). We nearly choked on our glasses of warm vintage Château Excel. Uncle Rick, we just didn't know you cared...

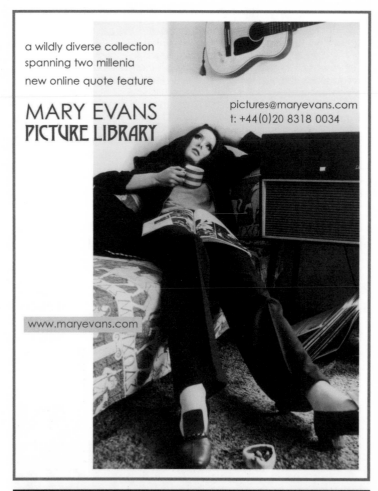

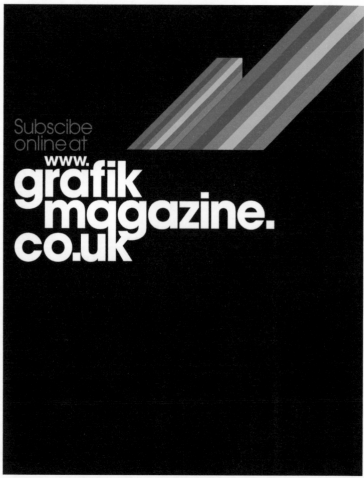

Rainbow Warrior.

Free entry and an amble through the park are just two of the reasons why you should make your way to the Serpentine Gallery this spring: the main one being the Ellsworth Kelly exhibition, which runs till 21 May. Kelly invented a vocabulary that is both rigorously spare and elegant and his abstract aesthetic is considered by many to be a precursor of the minimalist art of the 60s. The exhibition features recent paintings, sculptures and reliefs completed since 2002 that will be shown together for the first time. More details available at www.serpentinegallery.org

Light Fantastic.

Over the course of eight nights from 7–14 April, poetry becomes visual spectacle. As part of the Beckett Centenary Festival at the Barbican, American artist Jenny Holzer has been commissioned to design a series of light projections entitled For London. During her thirty-year career, Holzer has explored words as the material of her art. She began by writing her own texts; of late she has been increasingly drawn to the work of others, particularly those that touch upon universal, human themes. For more information about venues, dates and times for the projections visit www.barbican.org.uk

Listen Up. Stuck for inspiration?
Fear not, simply head for Scotland and for the latest in LongLunch's excellent series of design talks. This month's event takes place at The Lighthouse in Glasgow and features design gurus GTF. To reserve yourself a place at the LongLunch table on 20 April book now at www.longlunch.com

Keep the Faith.

Working across a range of media including print, wall drawing, video, sculpture and installation, Mark Titchner's work explores systems of belief, employing thought and writing from sources as diverse as the Old Testament, William Blake, Kabbalah and the Coca-Cola Corporation Manifesto. A show of his work at the Arnolfini Gallery which ends on 23 April, will feature a major new commission produced especially for the gallery. Take a closer look at www.arnolfini.org.uk

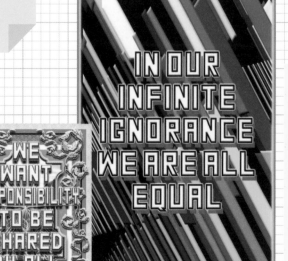

Roughs.

Bonjour Queens.

What better place for a visually enriching weekend away than Amsterdam where you can currently see a presentation of works by painter/designer Michel Quarez at the Stedelijk Museum. We definitely can't think of any. Born in 1938 in Damascus, Quarez trained in Paris at the Ecole Nationale Supérieure des Arts Décoratifs before heading off for a brief stint in New York, and eventually finding his way back to Paris. Quarez finds a lot of his themes in his immediate neighbourhood—the Paris suburb of Saint Denis—and his vibrant posters seem to ignore the edges of the paper on which they are printed. The exhibition runs at the Stedelijk till 21 May. Click on www.stedelijk.nl for more details.

All Mod Cons.

Searching for utopia? Well, you need look no further than the V&A's Modernism: Designing a New World exhibition, which begins on 6 April. Designed by London-based architect Eva Jiricna, it promises to be a colossal affair with over 300 objects and more than fifty film clips on show. Highlights include the earliest surviving fitted kitchen rarely exhibited drawings by Wassily Kandinsky and Harry Beck's first sketch for today's London Underground map. Quite an eyeful. For more details look up www.vam.ac.uk

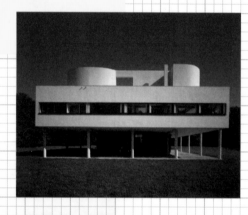

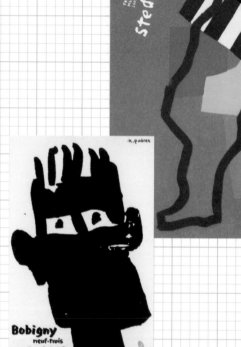

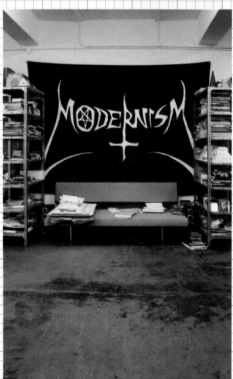

Dutch Delights.

This month feast your eyes on the work of the Dutch design geniuses that are Experimental Jetset at an upcoming exhibition featuring a selection of posters created by them over a ten- year period. The posters on display were produced between 1996–2006, and include work created while the Jetsetters were still studying at the Rietveld Academy. For your chance to sample a tasty slice of Dutch design, head down to the Kemistry Gallery in Shoreditch between 04 April and 30 May. More details available at www.kemistrygallery.co.uk

Go West. Lysergery at Westbourne Studios is a monthly event curated by Stuart Souter (A&R Warp Records) and Alexander Hutchins (assistant to Gavin Turk) that seeks to remedy the balance in West London's culturally barren landscape. But don't panic: despite the name there are no syringes or Botox involved here, only guest deejays live happenings and exciting visual art installations with the likes of Warp, Fat Cat, Domino, Twisted Nerve and DC Recordings. Visit www.westbournestudios.com to find out more.

SCAPING SERBIA

envy²

...luigi colani, ross lovegrove, karim rashid, konstantin grcic, peter saville, wieden and kennedy, roksanda ilinčić, davidoff, jan rijkenberg/bsur, slavimir stojanović, fernando gutierrez/pentagram, bruketa&žinić, metadesign, eugenio perazza/magis, designhotels, siniša vlajković, gaetano pesce, branko lukić, iaan bekker, maxim velcovsky, vladan srdić, diesel, kesselskramer, sicco van gelder, žaklina kušić, landor, deyan sudjic, kosta glušica, andrea klarin, ben evans, saša lakić, nicholas ind, miles newlyn...

100 of the best
6 festival days
5 top events
1 city: belgrade²

Amsterdam? Edinburgh? Been there, done that, got the stupid t-shirt. Question is, are you coming to the first Belgrade Design Week, from 17 until 22 April 2006?
So, want to envy² or be envied²?

www.belgradedesignweek.com

belgrade design week 2006

market² 17-18 April brand² 19-20 April design² 21-22 April beograd² 17-22 April fashion² 16-22 April

Posters by James Goggin Michael C. Place
Norm Rachel Thomas Non-Format RBG6
Laurent Fétis Alan Fletcher Experimental Jetset
Sanderson Bob Universal Everything
Frauke Stegmann Anthony Burrill Ryan Jones
John Morgan Angus Hyland Kerr|Noble
Jonathan Ellery Ceri Amphlett Deanne Cheuk
Daniel Eatock Adam Hayes Kim Hiorthøy
Ken Garland Designers Republic Damien Poulain
Antoine et Manuel Value and Service
Graphic Thought Facility Jonathan Schofield

grafik. LETRASET ULUVKĄ VODKA SEA

Felt-Tip catalogue out April 2006 Felt-Tip at
the London Design Festival September 2006
http://www.felt-tip.net

Design & Art Direction—Value and Service. Photography—Richard Learoyd.

Subscribe to Grafik
Graphic design/Art/Typography/Photography
Fashion/Books/Exhibitions/Ideas/Talent
From around the world to your door every month.

www.grafikmagazine.co.uk
Phone 0870 428 7957

Caffé
Cherry
Lampone
Vermiglione
Arancio
Bruno
Paglierino
Sabbia
Miele
Limone
Giallo Oro
Lime
Verde
Verde Pino
Smeraldo
Turchese
Blu
Dark Blue
Celeste
Perla
Nero

Sirio

21 rich colours, 80–700g, unlimited possibilities

For sales, information, swatches and samples:

Telephone 01604 820820
Fax 01604 844093
E-mail info@fedrigoni.co.uk

FEDRIGONI·UK

Fedrigoni UK is part of the Fedrigoni Group,
manufacturers of high quality papers and boards
distributed to over 60 countries worldwide.

Picture Post. [01]

Every day, in the wee small hours, while you're still slumbering safely in your bed, there's a massive national workforce mobilising to deliver your post. The Royal Mail's army of posties gets a pretty interesting view of the rest of us as it goes about its rounds. Photographer Stephen Gill wanted to produce a collection of photographs that draw on this postie's-eye view of the country so he joined forces with the Royal Mail and gave disposable cameras to two thousand of its postmen and women to record their lives. "No one photographer could ever have managed such a sweeping study of the country," says Gill. With images from the length and breadth of Britain, at all times of day, from cities to the countryside, this truly is an unprecedented portrait of a nation.

Gill's job was that of editor, spending time poring over every single image submitted and sorting them into categories until eventually the thousands of shots were whittled down to a book's worth, to which Gill has brought his keenly developed sense of pace and distinctive wit. The book has been designed by Gill's regular collaborator, Melanie Mues. "For the design I've decided to follow my initial instinct to keep the book simple," says Mues. "I didn't want the relatively complex administrative quest behind this project to show at any point. The presentation of the photographs was always going to focus on looking as down-to-earth and professional as possible. I treated each photograph with respect as I would with works by famous artists."

Showcase.

I Am a Camera. [02]

Dance-music darlings Layo and Bushwacka! launched their third and critically acclaimed album in March. For those familiar with the duo's sound, Feels Closer marks something of a sonic departure and the album represents a foray into new territory for the album's sleeve designers too. Yes, MadeThought has entered the world of sleeve design. The journey began when the London studio was asked to design an identity for Layo and Bushwacka!'s new record label, Olmeto, which led to a lively photoshoot in the studio of photographer Richard Learoyd and ended up with the finished sleeve you see here.

In typically recherché style, MadeThought approached the sleeve not as a one-dimensional object but as a chance to create the entry point into a whole world of graphic elements. "We thought it would be interesting if the album artwork physically existed in a space, and not just as digital artwork," explains MadeThought's Tom Crabtree. "We went about designing and producing poster-sized vinyl graphics containing all album information and credits and applied these to the walls and floor of a studio space. Also included in the installation were various objects of personal significance to the artists." The result is a memorable sleeve with graphic depth of field that embeds the album's identity in a graphic universe.

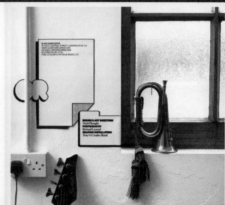

Stephen Gill
www.stephengill.co.uk
Mues Design
www.muesdesign.com
MadeThought
www.madethought.com
Olmeto Records
www.olmetorecords.com

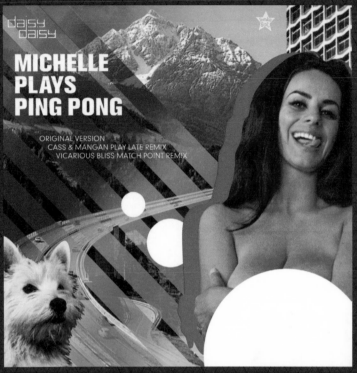

daisy
daisy

MICHELLE
PLAYS
PING PONG

ORIGINAL VERSION
CASS & MANGAN PLAY LATE REMIX
VICARIOUS BLISS MATCH POINT REMIX

PAM Airs. [03]

PAM's three protagonists—Paul (Plowman), Anthony (Burrill) and Malcolm (Goldie)—make "kinetic pictures with noises". Its latest masterpiece is the video and 12" sleeve for Daisy Daisy's single Michelle Plays Ping Pong (Sunday Best Recordings). It's certainly kinetic—in fact, Michelle is positively pneumatic and, dare we say it, even a little pornographic. While your ears are treated to a gentle but climactic buffing by Daisy Daisy, whose track is modelled around the rhythmic crescendos of a ping-pong ball's 'boink', PAM's visuals take your eyeballs on a Freudian romp through colour-saturated scenes of the Swiss Alps and mesmerising psychedelic kaleidoscopes. When the track is over you come round with a jolt to find yourself goggle-eyed, dribbling slightly and wondering where

the last three minutes disappeared to. It's hypnotic stuff. But don't take our word for it, see the vid yourself at www.daisydaisy.com. We'll leave you with a short introduction from PAM: "Michelle plays ping pong. Lots of it. She could have been an Olympic Gold medallist but she prefers to keep out of the spotlight, hustling in the basement clubs and bars of Paris where she lives. Notoriously talented, she plays with men or women, but none of them can survive her blistering forehand. By the time the game's over, they are reduced to a panting sweaty mess. A longtime fan of underground ping pong, Daisy Daisy finds himself watching Michelle thrashing girl after girl in the early hours... The noise he hears sparks an idea in his musical imagination. Racing back to his sonic laboratory, he mans the samplers and sets to work: 'Michelle Plays Ping Pong' is born'."

Showcase.

DEUTSCHE
BÖRSE
PHOTOGRAPHY
PRIZE
2006
ROBERT ADAMS
YTO BARRADA
PHIL COLLINS
ALEC SOTH

PHOTOGRAPHY
PRIZE
2006
ROBERT ADAMS
YTO BARRADA
PHIL COLLINS
ALEC SOTH

Top Spin. [04]

The Photographers' Gallery's annual Deutsche Börse Photography Prize (formerly the Citigroup Prize) rewards the living photographer who has produced the most exceptional work within the last twelve months. 2006 is a special year for the prize, being its tenth anniversary, and to mark the occasion the Photographers' Gallery has produced a special commemorative catalogue looking back at past winners to go alongside this year's winners' catalogue. London design agency Spin continues its sterling work in supplying the graphic material for the prize. "Our aim this year," says Spin's Joe Burrin, "was to be more expressive and playful with the imagery...

However, we retained the size of last year's catalogue and developed the logotype, using an outline to accentuate the text hierarchy. A new monospace font (Letter Gothic) was also introduced as the text face to complement the rounded forms of the logotype." The soft-back book has a dust jacket in four variations (one for each artist). The text on the cover is overprinted in a UV gloss varnish, "giving it", as Burrin describes, "the impression of a title-less book". This also leaves the imagery undisturbed and completes the entire catalogue's emphasis on the artist as individual: each photographer has a section in the book, which is introduced by a stock change, making it feel almost like four whole books in one.

PAM
www.paulanthonymalcolm.
com
Daisy Daisy
www.daisydaisy.com
Sunday Best
www.sundaybest.net
Spin
www.spin.co.uk
Photographers' Gallery
www.photonet.org.uk

Reduction Technique.

Robert Ryman is a painter in the truest sense of the word—his work explores the materiality of paint itself and the act of laying it on canvas and calling it art, all without the merest whiff of representing anything other than the paint itself. In recent years we have managed to release ourselves from the notion that painting cannot recover from such a moment of existentialism, and painters have re-emerged perforce. Thus, late 2005 was an apt moment for an exhibition of Ryman's work. In November and December the Xavier Hufkens Gallery in Brussels staged a show of Ryman's canvases from the mid-1960s and 2005. The catalogue has been designed by London designer William Hall and is the first in a series that he is to produce for the gallery.

I got to know Bob Ryman when he came to visit me in Amsterdam in the fall of 1969, after the opening of his first exhibition at the Konrad Fischer Gallery in Düsseldorf. Artists didn't have money for hotels in those days, so when 'on the road' they usually relied on the hospitality of local fellow-artists. Bob, who was quiet and introvert, opened up a little more each day and felt increasingly relaxed, and by the time he left a few days later, we'd mapped out all our ideas, predilections and passions about art. What remained was a lifelong friendship.

Neither Bob nor I is a great letter-writer, but when I went to New York for the first time a short while later, he picked me up at the airport. I stayed in his studio on the Bowery, a depressing boulevard in those days with a lot of alcoholics sleeping in the porticos.

I had a wonderful time…a loft to myself, the back of the studio filled with Bob's paintings, all types and sizes, older works, new ones. I was amazed that someone who had once been a passionate musician had, completely of his own accord, with no intermediary steps, discovered this art of painting. And that right from the beginning, with his very first attempts, he had produced paintings that were all unmistakably 'Rymans'. Each in its own right was imbued with that wonder about all the possibilities of paint as a material.

Bob had just moved in with his new love, the painter Merrill Wagner, about whom he'd spoken in Amsterdam. The first night they took me out to an enormous restaurant in the area, called 'Luchow's', a Bavarian-like sauerkraut palace the size of a factory with waitresses in dirndls and musicians in lederhosen. It was a fabulous evening!

But the highlight of that first trip as I recall it was Bob and Merrill's wedding reception in the posh Plaza Hotel, in the double suite of one of Merrill's old aunts, who was lying there sick in bed. After arriving, everyone shook her hand first and then, following a brief chat at her bedside, went to the other

room, which was filled with family and friends, white-gloved waiters and a bar-on-wheels. One of the gifts was a life-sized Steiff polar bear (white on white) that must have cost more than Bob and Merrill had earned in their whole lives up till then.

Bob has always had a very unique view of art, a mindful admiration, such as for Franz Kline, Rothko and Malevich, but sometimes also for strange things. For example, when my exhibition was being installed at the Guggenheim Museum in New York, and he pointed to a scratch in a white frame, saying he found that unexpected addition 'interesting'. He was clearly disappointed when I told him it had—annoyingly—been damaged.

I returned to New York many times after that. By then the hotels were paid for by the galleries or museums or the artists themselves, but I always made a visit to Bob's studio. Over the years, as one of the first I witnessed the birth of many beautiful paintings in that calm oasis on Greenwich Street, where his studio was now located.

I've intuitively admired Bob's work from the very beginning. All those different structures, those variations in material, that rare intensity and aura, those precisely placed screws, fasteners and holders, those lovingly prepared surfaces—from granular to smooth—those countless little squiggles of white paint, white in every conceivable hue, always radiant and highly luminous, those long drawn-out lines of the brush. We didn't need a lot of words, but I always left his studio feeling excited.

Bob doesn't say much about his work in public, but no one has captured better or more succinctly than he himself what his work is all about: 'There is never a question of what to paint, but only how to paint. The how of painting has always been the image.' That's Bob Ryman to the letter!

Jan Dibbets
San Casciano dei Bagni, 2005

"Ryman's paintings are exercises in control and reduction. Invariably using a square format and white paint, he sensitively explores brushwork, surface and materials," says Hall. "Such a refined collection of work required a delicate response which allowed the paintings visual space." Hall's treatment of the images is appropriately minimal, with each spread featuring a single image in isolation. The typographic treatment is equally restrained, with one size and weight of Akzidenz Grotesk used throughout. The cover, which is linen-bound and features the artist's first name on the back and his second name on the front, evokes the tactile qualities of the canvas that are such an important feature of Ryman's work.

William Hall
www.williamhall.co.uk
Tappin Gofton
www.tappingofton.com

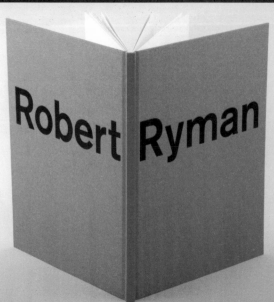

Showcase.

Drawing Room.

We live in a culture of such pronounced disposability that we dump computer monitors on the pavement, manufacture products with built-in obsolescence and support a whole 'entertainment' industry based on prostituting the dubious talents of fame-hungry wannabes farmed for an album's worth of cash, catapulted on a trajectory through the favours of gossip magazines, and then hustled out of the stage door to be replaced by a younger, more naïve model. So, no wonder music-makers such as band Morning Runner are determined to project a bit of longevity and credibility and distance themselves visually from the mass-produced aesthetic of the more disposable acts with whom they share the Top 40 shelf in HMV.

The artwork for Morning Runner's debut album was designed by London studio Tappin Gofton. It wholeheartedly eschews the album-artwork-by-numbers approach of cheesy band photograph and restrained typography in favour of virtuoso Victoriana illustrations by Kam Tang. "Initial conversations with the band," say the designers, "led us to a hand-made aesthetic and strong sense of craftwork. The final direction was inspired by a small collection of Victorian book illustrations from the British Library and the V&A." Kam Tang's delicate and ornate drawing for the album cover tells a romantic story in pictures and with individual scenes reworked as vignettes for the singles. The level of detail in Tang's drawings is sublimely suffocating and the artwork clamours for recognition in a way that would make any self-respecting Victorian heroine swoon with pride.

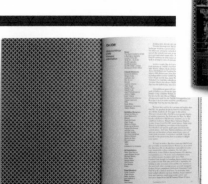

Costume Gallery. [07]

British Victorian neo-classical sculptor John Gibson has provided the inspiration for London's Studio Thomson and its work for the latest and fifth On | Off season at the Royal Academy. The much-vaunted On | Off runs at the venerable institution during London Fashion Week. Its mission is to place fashion by both emerging and established designers in a wider design context, and champion British design and manufacturing. During On | Off the Royal Academy plays host to catwalk displays as well as installations of product and interior design and fashion-tastic events. Each season Studio Thomson's sensitive and considered work for On | Off's brochure and invites provides the missing graphic design link.

For February 2006 Studio Thomson's concept came from Gibson's sculpture Narcissus, created in 1838. Photographer Paul Highnam captured the sculpture's androgynous beauty and a close crop of the face was used for the invite and cover. This approach was then echoed for all the living, breathing cast of On | Off. "Concentrating on the face and not the clothes," explains Studio Thompson, "we took thirty black and white portraits of the designers, artists and organisers, to form our own study of beauty in this era." Alongside these portraits (lit to emulate the way light bounces off marble statues such as Gibson's) is Studio Thomson's black and white fashion story set in the galleries and hallways of the Royal Academy. Thus, the whole brochure has a very definite sense of place, completed by endpapers decorated with a pattern inspired by Studio Thomson's studies of period archive books.

Showcase.

Swede Heart. ⁰⁸

Stockholm-based designer and art director Stefania Malmsten has designed the print campaign, catalogues, lookbooks and promotional material for Rodebjer's SS05 and AW06 collections. Malmsten has worked with New York-trained fellow Swede Carin Rodebjer for several seasons. The careers of both have flourished, with the fashion designer picking up several awards (including twice being named Elle magazine's designer of the year) and the graphic designer working on many prestigious projects for clients including Vogue Homme and Stockholm's Moderna Museet.

Featuring photographs by Andeas Larsson, Tove Falk Olsson and Thomas Klemetsson, Malmsten's work for Rodebjer is sophisticated and accomplished. But this refinement glides along on the back of Malmsten's subtle edginess. She often uses film in her work and the Rodebjer project is no exception, incorporating stills from a film shot on 16mm in collaboration with Göran Olsson.

Studio Thomson
www.studiothomson.com
Stefania Malmsten
www.stefania.se
Rodebjer
www.rodebjer.com

Animatronics.

The Musée d'Art Moderne Grand-Duc Jean (MUDAM) in Luxembourg supports an interesting programme of contemporary art- and graphic design-related works and projects. Recently it screened a series of animated films by designer Paul Kirps. Autoreverse is a collection of five short films depicting hybrid machines made from parts of domestic and office appliances, folding, opening and reassembling in a slightly sinister fashion, all to a soundtrack of beeps, whirs and clicks composed by the artist.

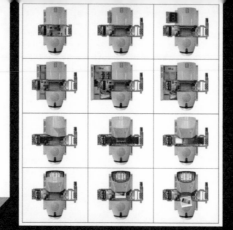

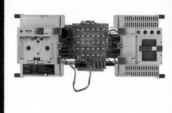

This is graphic designer Kirps's first foray into audio-visual work but it fulfils an attraction to machines that he's nurtured since childhood. "I am realising the dream of a little boy," he says. "At that time I always wanted to open televisions to see inside. This cost me some electric shocks." To create Autoreverse Kirps stockpiled a range of objects from cameras to radios to sewing machines, which he photographed from all angles. Then, using 3D animation, Kirps reconstituted the machines into fantastical hybrids. The films are available as limited-edition DVDs from the museum.

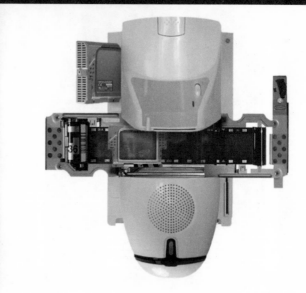

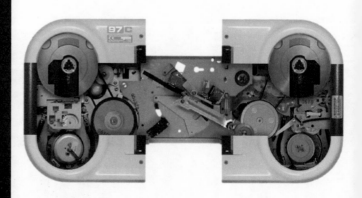

Showcase.

Kid Rock. [10]

Young musical whipper-snappers the Maccabees release their new single, Latchmere, on Fierce Panda Records on 10 April. The popular, fast-paced Brighton combo is already hot on the heels of its heroes, having supported the Strokes at a gig in their home town in January. The new release is accompanied by a video, conceived, designed and art-directed by fellow Brightonians Hugh Frost and Sam Bebbington, with photography by Holly Blake. The designers exploit the small-budget scale of their enterprise to great effect, composing the film from choppy animated sequences of still photography. Hugh Frost explains the thinking behind the sequence's narrative and style:

"The song is about the small things in life which are important, such as memories of Latchmere swimming pool, where members of the band first learned to swim, hence the pool tile-themed paper animations buzzing around on the back wall. Fans of the band were invited to show up for the shoot and bring an object that was important to them, all of which were then shot spinning in each of their hands as 100 people emerge from the studio cupboard." There is an air of great energy in this video that befits the music and is a tribute to its makers' burgeoning skills. The designers work under the moniker Posikids! and the motto "We don't know what we're doing, but we're not jaded yet" These kids have got gumption.

Paul Kirps
paakirps@pt.lu
MUDAM
www.mudam.lu
Posikids!
www.posikids.org
The Maccabees
www.themaccabees.co.uk

Peak Time. [11]

The most interesting digital arts festival in the UK is Lovebytes: for one, it takes place outside the capital, which means it taps into work you might not otherwise see, while also attracting the top talent from the field. Lovebytes 2006 took place in March and included customary input from Sheffield-dweller Matt Pyke of Universal Everything, who designs a yearly festival identity, curates a video gallery in the festival and advises on new content. The theme for this year's selection of works was 'environments' and this informed Pyke's approach to the identity.

He didn't have to look far from home for one of the most beautiful environments in the world—the Peak District. The region has been an inspiration to some of the greatest British landscape painters for 200 years and more now, but Pyke has dragged the notion of landscape painting wholeheartedly into the twenty-first century with, as he says, "a process/system-based approach" to the genre. "The landscape series," he continues, "was created from a single line to be printed on a pen-plotter... Each visual started with a flat landscape, which was then 'grown' into peaks, valleys and forests." The resulting short animation and stills form an identity that sums up the 'environments' theme of the festival, references it in its Sheffield location and also sets the bar for the high standard of work it showcases.

Universal Everything
www.universaleverything.com
Lovebytes
www.lovebytes.org.uk
Big Active
www.bigactive.com

Showcase.

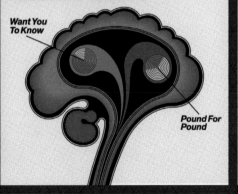

THE FREELANCE HELLRAISER

Want You To Know

Pound For Pound

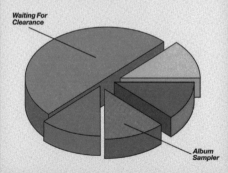

THE FREELANCE HELLRAISER

Waiting For Clearance

Album Sampler

Hell, Yes. [12]

Another admirable sleeve from the Big Active camp comes this month in the form of its designs for The Freelance Hellraiser's new album. The DJ and producer, aka Roy Kerr, is impeccable in his creative references, having named himself after the original freelance hellraiser—and Grafik's favourite roguish thespian—Oliver Reed (any man who can inspire the legend of performing one-armed press-ups on the bar over which he has just consumed twenty pints of Best is all right by us). And Kerr's music isn't bad either. He's better known for his remix of Christina Aguilera's A Stroke of Genius and his work with The Editors and Placebo, though, and this is Kerr's first solo outing. Gerard Saint of Big Active explains the visual approach for The Freelance Hellraiser:

"The bold info-diagrammatic look we have created for his first single and album promo is indicative of the style we are developing over the campaign. The idea is to create a twisted series of graphics that wouldn't look out of place in a vintage copy of Graphis Diagrams, but with random and hidden meanings that can only be worked out through clues in the music. Both CD formats are produced as uncoated capacity wallets to enhance the feel of the graphics." Right, then, who's getting the first round in?

THE FREELANCE HELLRAISER

Waiting For Clearance

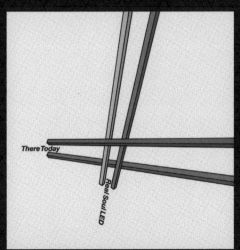

There Today

Real Soul LED

01

02

Material World.

The TextielLAB at the Textielmuseum in Tilburg is a fully-functioning R&D resource that's used by many of Holland's best textile designers. When Merkx+Girod Architects were appointed to give it a makeover, they asked typeface designer René Knip to create a special graphic language for the space. Here, M+G's Bas Berck explains how they went about it.

Who?

In the last couple of years we have designed several landmark exhibitions in the Netherlands including The Glory of the Golden Age and Masterpieces, both at the Rijksmuseum, Amsterdam, and Morocco, 5000 Years of Culture, in the New Church in Amsterdam. Besides designing these elaborate exhibitions we have also accumulated large experience in designing interiors for important Dutch architectural monuments such as the Concertgebouw (concert hall) in Amsterdam and the Inktpot building in Utrecht. This quite rare combination of experience and skills has inspired the Dutch Textielmuseum in Tilburg to invite us to design the new interior of the TextielLAB within its monumental museum building, a former textile factory.

What?

Merkx+Girod Architects were especially interested in 'celebrating' the monumental factory environment and in emphasising (not denying) its specific atmosphere, materials, colours and architectural details. M+G thus decided to create an exhibition and working area within the factory envelope that touched no walls. In order to do this, a giant steel 'carpet' was designed and engineered which at certain points becomes three-dimensional when it is folded upright. The carpet organises and demarcates the various textile techniques on display, such as preparation, weaving, knitting, tufting and embroidering, into separate areas. This steel environment blends in with the machine language and has clear graphic elements added such as green 'stitch seams' indicating visitor routes and dividing the go and no-go areas.

All the different textile techniques are still in use and the TextielLAB thus functions as a research playground for many Dutch (textile) designers who can spend R&D periods at the museum (by invitation), often resulting in new exhibitions at the museum. This also means the TextielLAB is not a 'dead museum' but a fully functioning and living interior space which is used intensively and visited daily. For each textile technique a separate working area has been designed by M+G. These bright green furniture pieces consist of tailor-made wooden desks and shelves, seamlessly covered with a green latex skin. Large display cupboards are made from various types of wood with different textures and colours that have been 'woven together'.

Dutch graphic designer René Knip, with whom M+G had previously worked on several projects, was asked to develop a special language for all the graphic items present. Knip used the existing language of textile techniques, like embroidery, to create text and letters with. This resulted in an appropriate typographic treatment for each textile technique. Large colourful words on transparent screens like WEVEN (weaving) and BORDUREN (embroidery) are placed strategically above the corresponding area. The old 'Bazenhok' (boss's office) is now used for computer design and preparations and has been fitted with a bright graphic wall showing the text "TextielLAB, develop and discuss". At several points within the exhibition visitors may consult computer screens which offer interactive information about the various techniques, what's on and which designers are currently working at the TextielLAB. All these computers have also been integrated with the steel floor.

03

04

05 TEXTIELLAB

01

How?

The Dutch steel construction and engineering company Bronnenberg created a special apparatus to place the extremely heavy steel carpet elements exactly in place. This millimetre-precision job went without any hitches and was unprecedented. The entire interior design was realised without any problems and is considered to have been very successful, judging by the positive reactions and high numbers of visitors. The TextielLAB was also nominated for the Annual Dutch Design Prize in 2005.

Why?

See above.

Specification?

Dutch Textile Museum, Tilburg. Start of project: 2004. Realisation: mid-2005. Project duration: one year. Project team: Evelyne Merkx, Patrice Girod, Jan Willem Wijker, Det van Oers, Bert de Munnik, Josje Kuiper and Sanne Oomen. Total area: 890 m². Various materials used: e.g. steel, wood covered in latex, wood-woven cabinets, glass and graphics.

02

03

04

BORDUREN

01　Poster designed
　　by René Knip
02, 03
　　TextielLAB interior
　　Photo courtesy of
　　Roos Aldershoff
04　Custom typeface
　　designed by René Knip
05　Plexiglass singage
　　designed by René Knip

www.merkx-girod.nl
www.textielmuseum.nl
www.atelierreneknip.nl

05

Profile
Daniel Eatock

Text by Jonathan Bell

02

01
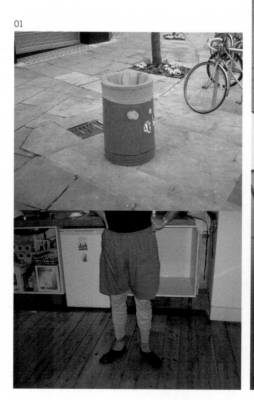

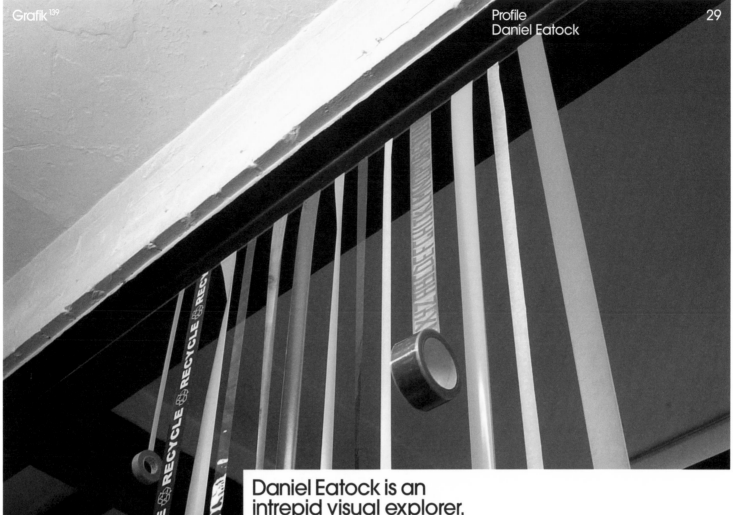

03

Daniel Eatock is an intrepid visual explorer, reporting back to the rest of us via list-making, documentary photography, obsessive visual quantification and playful experiments. Oh, and he does a bit of graphic design too. <u>Jonathan Bell</u> met him to get the Eatock story and discussed everything from his successfully non-commercial approach to the art of balancing on two chair legs.

Our culture overflows with visual information, much of it superfluous, so perhaps we should be thankful that the vast majority of 'design' doesn't persist; it simply gets scrumpled up and recycled, peels off and fades away. This isn't Daniel Eatock's way. In the past decade the designer has created a sizeable body of work, both on his own and in collaboration with others, all of which is exhaustively chronicled on his website (www.eatock.com). Nothing disappears.

Eatock remains best known for two quite disparate projects, one personal, one commissioned. His modest Greeting Card series, sold through his website, presents the card writer with a checklist of options—significant birthdays, recipients, etc: a system that demands intervention. "I wanted to design a range that could accommodate every need for cards, but then the user could add their own element," he says. Like any original idea, the concept has spawned a huge number of (lesser) imitators, yet Eatock's originals retain an unequalled simplicity. The physical form of each Greeting Card is determined by the information it contains—instructions, format, text and content—all pragmatically arranged in a fashion that suggests Eatock has no time for self-conscious design. The other principal client in his portfolio is Channel 4, with whom Eatock enjoys a fertile creative partnership, producing a type-driven visual identity that had become synonymous with a suite of the channel's most recognisable programmes of the early twenty-first century, along with the 'eye' symbol that has accompanied the various series of Big Brother.

Eatock's approach is varied yet contains several unified themes. After studying at Ravensbourne, Eatock graduated from the RCA in 1998, having taken a deliberately non-commercial approach throughout his course. He belongs to the tail of the generation who studied during the transitional period between analogue and digital, with the result that he takes neither method for granted. "All my work starts with pen and paper—I've never worked quick enough on the computer," he says. Despite his studio's dependence on the internet as a means of maintaining a database of past works, Eatock retains a very analogue edge, at odds with the fashion for slick, layered digital work that predominated in the tail-end of the Nineties. This style did not appeal. "I was so desperate not to get a job in a graphic design studio, both before and after the RCA," he recalls, and describes his relief at securing an internship at Minneapolis's Walker Art Center under the curatorship of Andrew Blauvelt.

His time at the Walker was to prove very fruitful. "It was almost like a perfect extension to the RCA... working for the curators and artists. It was a way that I could test my own work in a real situation," says Eatock, and the Walker's extensive programme of exhibitions and publications gave him a wide variety of scenarios and briefs to experiment with. "Once that had finished I'd done everything I could do in graphic design—the work volume was exhaustive," he says. On his return to London he did little straight design work, preferring to teach and to build furniture with architect Sam Solhaug; the two set up Foundation 33 to develop ideas that originated in long hours in the Walker's carpentry shop. It was at about this time that a chance meeting enabled Eatock to pitch for the Big Brother graphic identity (although he'd missed the first series by being in the USA). "I won that pitch, although I had quite radical ideas, then ever since I've done projects for Channel 4... it's a perfect way to do other work, as the Channel 4 work supported the studio." Foundation 33 was eventually subsumed into Boymeetsgirl, an "interdisciplinary creative agency" founded in 2004 by Andy Law and Kate Stanners. Eatock became the design director, a relatively short-lived post that gave him "an insight into the very different world of advertising".

02

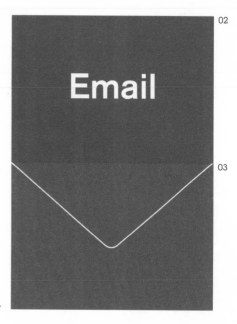

03

01

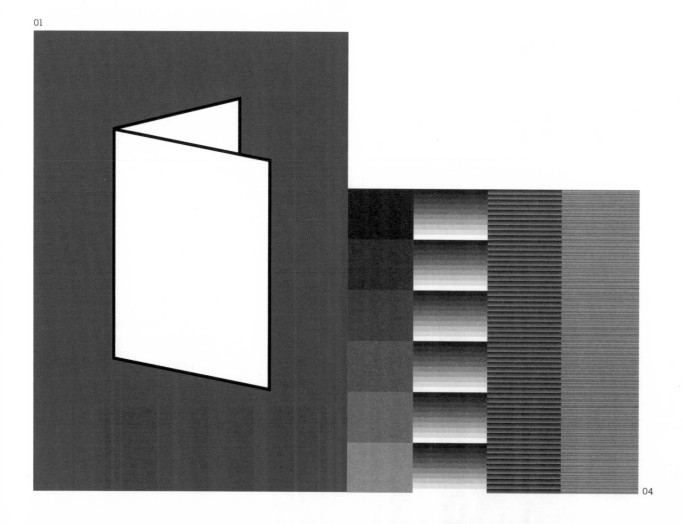

04

Junk Mail

this postcard is temporarily
out of stock

I would like to know how many nightlight candles I can light before the first one burns out

I would like to make the smallest ton

I would like to eat lots of garlic then blow up children's party balloons

01

02

04

03
Entrepreneurial Authorship

Alongside commissioned projects I am
interested in presenting ideas that are
conceptual and that have not been applied in a
commercial context. Following are a few ideas
and suggestions to whom they may be relevant:

An idea for a drinks company

I would like to pour a complete bottle/can of
water/olive oil/orange juice etc. in one
continuous stream from a pre calculated height,
and take a single photograph before the first
drip hits the ground.

An idea for a skateboard manufacture

I would like to make a skateboard coated with
Blackboard paint that comes with pack of chalk
and a board duster. I would also like to make a
skateboard coated with a Whiteboard surface
that comes with pack of dry markers and a
board wipe.

An idea for a trainer/shoe manufacturer

I would like to replace the laces on a pair of
trainers/shoes with some very long ones, tie
them together and then throw them over a
telegraph wire so they hang down until they
almost touch the ground.

An idea for Heinz or another
similar food manufacture

I would like to mix together every single Heinz
food product, then package in small cans
labelled as a limited edition of everything Heinz.

An idea for a football team

I would like to get the team to wear plain white
t-shirts then stand in a line, I would then walk
around them spraying a continuous red line
across the fronts and backs of their t-shirts.

01

02

04

03

I would like to ask people what they are going to buy as they are walking into a supermarket and ask them what they bought on their way out.

I would like to make an archetypal steel ruler one kilometer long.

I would like to be asked to spell every word in the concise Oxford English Dictionary as a standard high school spelling test. I would form a list of all the words I spelt wrong a list of all the words I spelt correctly.

I would like to curate a show called 'Untitled' containing works that are all 'Untitled'.

I would like to buy postcards in art museums of artwork on display then hold them in front of the actual artwork and take a photograph.

I would like to write non stop for 24 hours

I would like to know how many night light candels I can light before the first on burns out.

I would like to copy every single artist signature from every artwork displayed in the Tate Modern on a single page.

I would like to own a complete set of Edward Ruscha's artist books.

I would like to cut all my t-shirts in half and have them stiched back together.

I would like to read every book I own.

I would like to meet Yoko Ono.

I would like to employ a professional proof reader to read through all my sketch books and proof corrections.

I would like to collaborate with 3m to make the Fly Post-it a mass passed artwork.

I would like to make the smallest ton.

I would like to see 1 ton of feathers.

I would like to open a can of Piero Manzoni merda.

I would like to add more paint to a real Picasso.

I would like to commission Sol Lewit to make a wall drawing on the celing.

I would like to ask Tracy Emin to make a bed.

I would like to hear Paul McCartney sing only John Lennon songs.

I would like to exhibit Richard Prince joke paintings at a comedy club.

I would like to own a John & Yoko war is over poster.

I would like to design a Royal mail postage stamp with a drawing of an envelope on it.

I would like to make blank badges for people to wear over the logos and brand marks on clothing.

I would like to hang paintings from the Renaissance in a gallery with the smell of fresh oil paint.

I would like to put an Alkerseltzer in a pint of beer.

I would like to have seen Andy Kaufman read The great Gatsby.

05

Grafik¹³⁹

Documentation and presentation are integral to the Eatock approach; projects tend to linger in their virtual folders long after the physical evidence of their existence has vanished. Either works chronicle passing moments or arrangements, most notably with the Picture of the Day series or the compositions of balancing objects, or they deal with editions, systems and series that seek out accidental or deliberate repetition. The latter forms the core of a work undertaken in September 2002 at the Whitechapel Gallery's Project Space: "the world's largest signed and numbered limited-edition artwork" involved ten people signing one million cards, all of which were then hand-stamped and distributed free. While The World's Largest addresses the profession's sometimes overly precious obsession with 'artist's editions', Eatock and his collaborators are also genuinely interested in the redemptive power of objects, a love of things that seeks to give even the humble postcard a place in your heart.

Twenty-first-century graphic design is increasingly characterised by its dissociation from the physical; for the most part, designers work using digital processes that may or may not result in a tangible object. Add to this the maniacal pace of cultural consumption, and nothing, it seems, sticks around for very long. Eatock is wading against this particular current, through his comprehensive website, through the numerous works that define a fixed point in space and preserve it, and through the studio's physical output. "I use the website kind of like a sketchbook—you can change it, it's not like printing a book," he says. "It's a constant document, updated often two... or three times a week." Although he claims not to "think about how to transform ephemeral things", Eatock acknowledges how his photography in particular is about catching a "fleeting moment", when two things come together, be they the miniature eclipse created by a streetlamp in front of the sun, or the deceptively casual observations depicted in Picture of the Week. These unvarnished, verbatim digital snaps are of editorial conceits, save an attempt to "centre the concept in the middle of the image". "It's not about the photographs, but more about the concepts—that's the moment, it becomes the work," he continues.

ABCDEFGHIJKLM
NOPQRSTUVWXYZ

06

01, 02, 05	Timecapstool
03	List
04	Burying Treasure
06	Alphabetape
07	Neckclasp

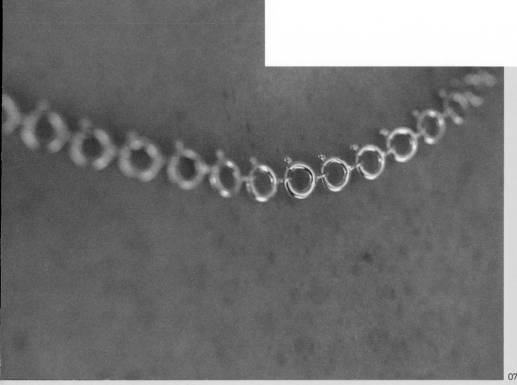

07

01

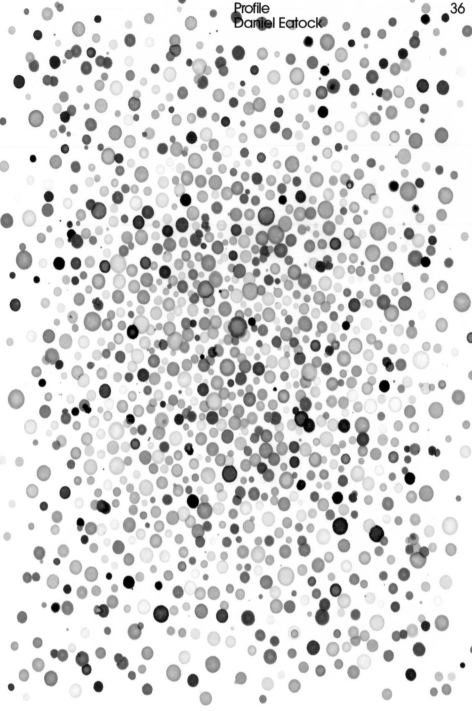

02

At the heart of Eatock Ltd's output is a dichotomy, a split between pragmatic visual honesty, straightforward typography, material simplicity and innate functionalism, and the sense that all is not what it seems. "I enjoy working with standard things and making them different," says Eatock. "I see traits that are evident in all the projects, such as A-size formats, and usually the same typeface [Akzidenz Grotesk]." These choices are deliberate. "I want to remove the subjectivity—choosing the font, paper size, colour," he says, "A limited palette is like a limited wardrobe—it saves time." Similarly, the image series, be they of car batteries, Father Christmases or damaged Fiat Coupés, generate their focus from the combination of repetition and subtle change. "The more of them you see, the more interesting they are," he says.

Meaning is never straightforward. His price-tag wrapping paper is playing a game— "Traditionally you don't want people to know the value; I wanted to show how ridiculous this convention was"—and the paper is festooned with hundreds of price tags of varying values. The ultimate meaning remains up for grabs: is this subverting our attempts to conceal how much a gift cost, or simply celebrating the sheer variety of price tags? Not all the projects share this ambiguity. "Some works are completely concluded," Eatock continues, citing One Stone—a stone weighing exactly one stone, which could be an "unlimited edition"— and the Neckclasp, a necklace formed solely from clasp fittings. "You can make a thing just by using fasteners—that's the perfect project for me. It's the perfect object; it's functional, beautiful." Other works revel in dual meanings. Alphabetape presents an alphabet embedded in a role of packing tape. "I was interested in the way people used tape to write with—I see it almost like a typeface," Eatock says. "It's not a digital font, but something you have to physically use." Hence difference and individuality come out of each application.

03

Some concepts come around again and again. Felt-Tip Print consists of a piece of paper balanced on the nibs of pens, a development of a college piece called Bleeding Art. The multi-coloured inks seep through the paper, creating a galaxy of coloured spots of varying sizes. "It connects completely to graphic design," Eatock remarks, pleasantly surprised, "although it's a new version of very old work." Other ideas branch off into unexpected avenues. Eatock's ongoing fascination with the tension and release of the balancing act has evolved from objects to form. Through the website he continues to solicit images of balanced stacks of mundane objects (although most, he notes dryly, are of desktop objects, books and stationery, as his website visitors turn their attention to their immediate environment for inspiration). "I never connected the physical part of balance with the aesthetic," he says. "I'm interested in watching skateboarders, for example, something that's really fluid, even dangerous, but also poetic." His current Chair Balance series is part-performance, part-nostalgia. "Balancing on the [Robin Day] chair reminded me of being a kid, but I didn't want to have a safety net," he says, explaining how he has worked the balancing act into his lectures, beginning each talk with the act of keeping the chair on its two spindly legs. "As I did more and more lectures I started drawing comparisons between physically balancing and composition—to balance relies on constant movement and adjustment. There's never really that perfect moment in the middle."

The sense of balance extends to social conventions. While at Boymeetsgirl, Eatock created My Favourite Cup, a subtly subversive response to the territorial nature of big offices. "I started to use other people's favourite cups, as a means of friendly antagonism—i.e. picking someone's favourite for your own cup of coffee and then casually taking it over to them for a chat," he says, "I made a couple of hundred cups [all printed with the words 'My Favourite Cup'] to try and unify people."

Most importantly, old and new projects continue to have a parallel existence, a central part of Eatock's philosophy. "With my new work I'm interested in letting the other work exist so that it can endure and perhaps have a different meaning," he says, with more recent works occupying the fuzzy boundary between art and design, deliberately evoking the heyday of minimalist and conceptual art. Eatock cites Lucy R. Lippard's Six Years: The Dematerialization of the Art Object as his favourite book. "It made me look at graphic design again, and I started to apply those ideas to design projects," he says, and there are clear parallels between his more site-specific and self-initiated works and the elements of repetition, cataloguing, archetypes and juxtapositions found in the works of Joseph Beuys, Sol LeWitt, Carl Andre et al.

Now back working largely on his own, his studio seems relaxed and happily immersed in personal work, as if the rude reality of commercial pressures are elsewhere. "I like juggling the two," Eatock admits, adding that he's "doing less and less of the Big Brother and Channel 4 work". Eatock is in the process of "exploring the relationship between my self-initiated projects and my commissions". Again, this approach suggests a tension, a need for balance and constant exploration. For now, this seems the right way forward. "I find this approach very comfortable," he acknowledges, before adding, almost unnecessarily, "but I have lots of contradictions."

05

01	Sun Light
02	Felt-Tip Print
03	Utilitarian greetings cards
04	Making of Felt-Tip Print
05	Bathroom Products Balanced

Eatock Ltd
7 Minerva Street
London E2 9EH
+44 (0)20 7739 0174
www.eatock.com

07

Matthew Barnes.

Modestly attributing his success to "lucking out", Barnes has found time, aside from his studies in Graphic Arts at the Liverpool School of Art and Design, to work for the likes of Content, Rockpile and Arkitip magazines. His greatest triumph, perhaps, has been the chance to immortalise his illustrations on a Nike Tyvek jacket as part of the brand's Performance Art exhibition, which will be displayed in stores around London. "I wanted to create something a bit psychedelic and surreal—something you'd probably never see printed on a jacket, and particularly not one by a huge sports brand." Barnes explains. "I don't think Nike have ever had Bavarians riding tigers and dogs on their clothes before," he adds genially.

Barnes's extracurricular activities also include package design for Smalltown America Records and a regular slot illustrating for Rockpile magazine, jobs which allow him to indulge in his other passion, music. In fact, it was as a record-obsessed twelve-year-old that Barnes first took an interest in design. "I started looking more at the layouts of sleeves and the way they were drawn and put together," he recalls. Indeed, it is this fascination with construction and reconstruction that forms the basis of much of Barnes's work. A fan of the punk aesthetic, he holds the cut'n'paste ideology dear, and combines hand processes with computer manipulation in order to achieve the layered and embellished feel of many of his illustrations. In this way, Rockpile collaborations have allowed Barnes the freedom to visually interpret music via manipulation and reillustration of photographs. "For example, the Devendra Banhart image was drawn in marker pen, scanned back in, and then altered and layered with other elements," he explains. "I usually look at the things I associate with the artist and then subvert it or play with it— for Banhart, I wanted a really ghostly, psychedelic, folky feel."

Aside from experiments with phonetic typography and deconstructed fashion imagery, it is Barnes's quirky portraiture that is most intriguing. "I try to remember people I've seen that day, those strange eccentric people who wander round every town and you're not entirely sure if they're real or just your imagination," he explains. "I get a bit of a kick out of taking people and making them odd-looking." So while Liverpool's bag ladies take heed, is there a key to Barnes's undergraduate triumph? "Keep your ear to the ground." It's as simple as that.

08

09

10

11

01 Design for Peace T-shirt
02, 03
    Deconstructed Fashion
04 Kaiser Chiefs illustration
    for Rockpile magazine
05, 06
    Images for Arkitip
    magazine, issue 31
07 Devendra Banhart
    illustration
08 Like, from Clockwork
    Illustration series
09 Matthew Barnes badges
10 Tyvek jacket for
    Performance Art exhibition
11 Spring
www.thebattle.co.uk
Profile by Laura Clayton

01

02

03

04

05

06

07

08

Jens Schildt.

After being simultaneously baffled by a rogue silkscreen frame left lying about and a vector drawing programme discovered on a friend's computer, Swedish graphics whiz Jens Schildt decided he had better find out what this design lark was all about. That was over ten years ago, and he has since ditched his day job to study at Amsterdam's prestigious Rietveld Academy where he has not only produced some rather nice work, but has also discovered a taste for "polite society".

Lauding the international environment Rietveld offers, Schildt explains: "I think it's necessary to have a multilingual and multicultural climate in art schools. That way, they can then work as a role model towards a more courteous society." Indeed, it is such political and social awareness that influences much of Schildt's work. Take, for example, Re-Create No.1, a project in which Schildt—disheartened by the number of advertisements found on houses in Amsterdam—replaced the posters on a building with his own designs, intended to re-create and reclaim the original appearance of the structure's walls. "For each A0 poster I made eight A3 colour prints and glued them together on a sheet of paper," he reveals. He then produced a magazine to document his public intervention: "It stayed for almost a week until they put up the new ads again."

Not content with championing urban regeneration, Schildt is also concerned with European cultural values. He has produced packets of stickers and accompanying publicity which aim to promote an increase in government spending on culture from 7 cents per citizen to 70 cents each year. "The idea is to hand out stickers to be put on coins which can then be distributed throughout Europe," Schildt explains. Whether or not you can persuade a cashier to go along with this when you present your orange coins is another matter entirely.

However, it's not just social issues which get Schildt going—he's also a self-professed rock 'n' roll fanatic who gets his kicks playing in his band, Super Cricket, designing record sleeves and creating the odd personal fanzine "existing in one copy only" dedicated to his idol, Roky Erickson, of 60s psychedelia band the Elevators.

So what does the future hold for Schildt? "I hope I can find nice people to work with and that all the nice people I already know will still be nice and that everybody can be respectful and considerate of other people, all together in Our Polite Society." Of course.

09

11

10

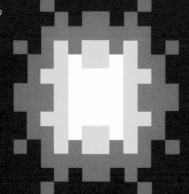

Special
Report—Play.

Block
Head.

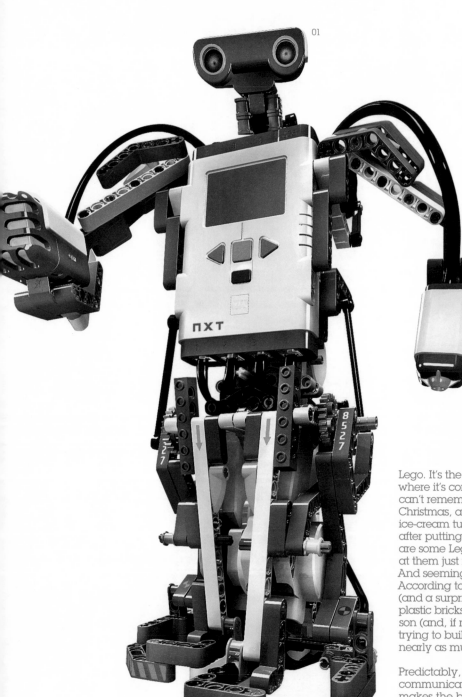

01

For many of us, the little red, yellow and blue blocks of Lego were one of the first toys that we really engaged with. Now in its seventy-fourth year, the company is still going strong, embracing the likes of Star Wars and Harry Potter and about to launch a new range of Bluetooth-enabled Lego robots. Here Grant Gibson finds out more about Denmark's biggest export.

Lego. It's the playroom equivalent of bindweed—you never know where it's come from but it always seems to be there. As a child I can't remember buying any, or even unwrapping a boxful at Christmas, and yet there was always a stack of it stored in an old ice-cream tub at the bottom of my play box. I sat down to write this after putting my three-year-old son to bed and, sure enough, there are some Lego Duplo blocks in the corner of his room. I was looking at them just now, trying to work out when on earth they'd arrived. And seemingly I'm not alone—Lego is genuinely ubiquitous. According to the company's website, more than 400 million children (and a surprising number of adults) will play with its six-studded plastic bricks this year alone. But what's the attraction? Well, for my son (and, if memory serves, his father) it's all about destruction. Yes, trying to build a tower as high as it would possibly go is OK but not nearly as much fun as smashing it to pieces afterwards.

Predictably, Charlotte Simonsen, Lego's head of corporate communications, has a rather more complex take. "I think what makes the brick evergreen is that it has the ability to make something systematic," she tells me. "It unites systematic thinking, creativity and role play—so you have a lot of things in one toy." A socially responsible plastic brick, of course, could only originate from one part of the world...

02

03

04

05

06

01	AlphaRex,
	Lego Mindstorms
02	Bionicle 8623
03	Star Wars 4492
04	Star Wars 4495
05	Knights' Kindom
06	Lego Technic 8435

Lego was founded in 1932 by carpenter Ole Kirk Christiansen in the village of Billund, Denmark, as a desperate measure. Like the rest of the Europe, Denmark's economy was still heavily depressed after the Wall Street Crash three years earlier and Christiansen's carpentry work had dried up. Crafting wooden toys for middle-class children was all that remained. Lego, which incidentally means 'I put together' in Latin, remains in family hands to this day. In 1947 it invested in a plastic injection-moulding machine and in 1949 it created the Automatic Binding Brick, a product that has proven almost completely fad-proof. It is, without doubt, one of Scandinavian modernism's most successful exports. However, unlike, say, IKEA, it has never attempted to brand itself as such. "We haven't defined ourselves like that," confirms Simonsen. "Our branding, our products are extremely international. Actually a lot of consumers don't know we're Danish." Not that surprising perhaps when you consider that the majority of Lego users are under ten, but you understand the sentiment.

With the exception of a sticky spell at the turn of the millennium, the company has always been remarkably light on its feet, both pandering to and steadfastly ignoring fashion. It has the happy knack of spotting the zeitgest (hence the licence agreements for Spider-Man, Manga and Batman) without ever becoming its slave. Even a cultural juggernaut like Star Wars somehow gets sucked into Lego's world, when many would expect the opposite to happen. Partly this has been down to product innovation—the company launched a line of robots in 1998 called Lego Mindstorms and its soon-to-be-released second generation will be Bluetooth-enabled—but also to its effective use of the internet. Simonsen describes the company's website as "a link between the product and the virtual world". Lego fanatics are encouraged to create new designs for an online competition, with the winner receiving royalties when the idea is put into production.

Ultimately the company and the brick it manufactures are inexorably linked and their success can be put down to flexibility. As its sales tag says, Lego offers "never-ending possibilities", a notion that's been explored by a number of artists. Most famously, in 1996, Polish sculptor Zbigniew Libera used the product to create a seven-box, limited-edition set of a concentration camp. While the packaging looked authentic enough, coming complete with the Lego logo, the bricks inside were uniformly grey, the figures, whose features had been manipulated, almost ghost-like. Photographs on the larger boxes showed Lego models with protruding ribs, being hanged under the watchful glare of an SS officer, or trapped forlornly behind barbed wire. The piece still has the power to shock nearly a decade on, proving how easy it is for any system—whether it's democracy or Lego—to be brutally subverted. When asked to comment on the piece, Libera enigmatically opined: "I am from Poland; I've been poisoned."

Naturally enough, after it was first shown Lego tried to sue and the artist himself was forced to withdraw from the 1997 Venice Biennale when he was asked by the curator of his national pavilion, Jan Stanislaw, not to show the piece.

01

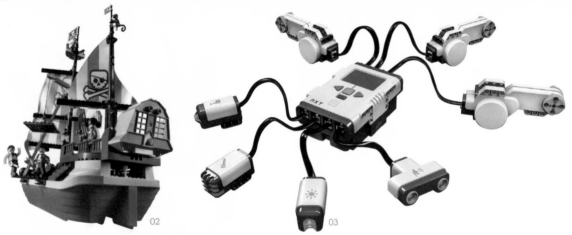

02   03

Libera isn't the only one fascinated by the product's potential. Closer to home, British duo Darren Neave and John Cake, otherwise known as the Little Artists, have carved themselves a place in the crowded contemporary art market by paying homage to other work in Lego. Starting in the mid-Nineties, they first came to attention with their miniature version of Damien Hirst's formaldehyde shark, before following it up five years later with Salvador Dalí's famous lobster phone. "We used to call it kitchentable art, where anything you had at home was great for making a sculpture out of. We weren't necessarily painters or traditional sculptors but it just felt right to be using Lego," says Cake now.

The Little Artists' fascination with Lego simply echoes the experience of millions of other adults around the world. "We've never stopped buying Lego, even when we were ten and eleven and most people where getting into computer games or something," adds Cake a little conspiratorially. "We bought it secretly and we've always updated our Lego library." Very much aware of such patterns of behaviour, the company is looking to capitalise on this grown-up market. Lego Serious Play, for example, is a consultancy tool that attempts to help companies create new business systems using small plastic bricks. With the help of a consultant provided by Lego, firms are encouraged over a number of sessions to think out of the box—provided they can build one in the first place, presumably. According to Simonsen: "It's a way of moving your business into the future through Lego." Whether it will ever catch on in British boardrooms is open to question but it's certainly more original than various advertising agencies' habit of sticking a retro-computer game in the corner of the workplace in an attempt to look hip and relaxed.

So what of the future? Will children still be playing with plastic bricks in three generations' time? Simonsen thinks so. "We'll keep going on with the traditional bricks and traditional products because children will not stop playing with traditional toys. They'll want to play a physical game, they won't want to spend their whole time staring at screens." Certainly after a couple of difficult years, the firm seems to have come out of the doldrums by concentrating on what it describes as its "core product", and reining the brand back in. Under pressure from MP3 players and mobile phones as well as having prices squeezed by the retail giants, the traditional toy market is static but, having sold off some factories and its theme parks, Lego is back in the black. One senses as our architecture changes to incorporate new technology and building techniques, so will the bricks. It could be that in thirty years' time I'll be buying the Zaha Hadid Intelligent Building Set for my grandchildren, but, however it develops, I fancy there'll be some lingering around kids' play boxes for many years to come.

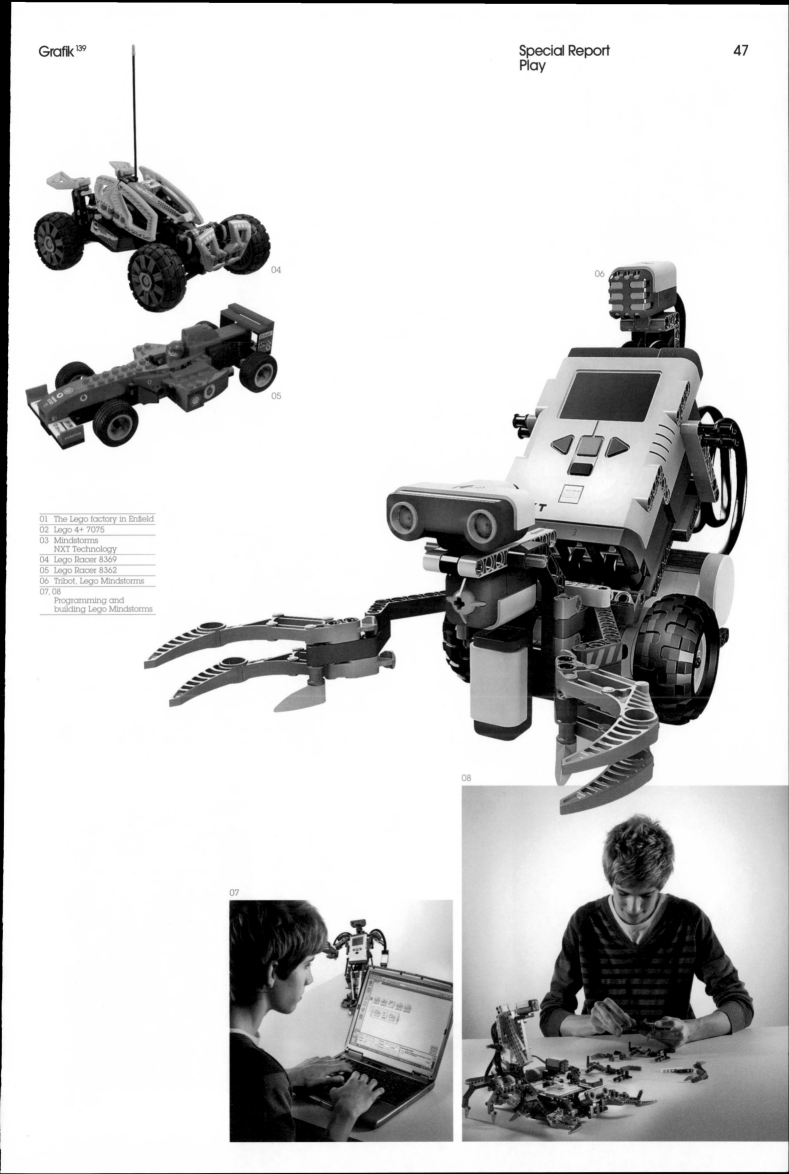

04

05

06

08

07

01

Love Shuffle.

The furtive glances, the mind games, the deft handiwork, and the satisfaction of coming first—playing cards have always been at the epicentre of social occasions. Here Angharad Lewis finds out about a deck of cards from underwear-makers Lascivious that's guaranteed to get you hot under the collar before you've even been dealt a hand.

02

03

01 ButtonBrothel
02 TADO
03 Cecilia Carlstedt
04 Satoshi Matsuzawa
05 Nadia Hunt
06 Nem/Shinji Nemoto
07 Cecilia Carlstedt

04

05

06

07

NADIA HUNT
nadiahunt@hotmail.com

SATOSHI MATSUZAWA
www.salboma.com

SHINJI NEMOTO
www.nineohm.com

CECILIA CARLSTEDT
www.agentform.se

From the Indian Karma Sutra to Playboy Bunnies, putting naughty pictures on playing
cards is nothing new. Cheap, handy and portable, a pack of playing cards is the perfect
visual vehicle for a spot of pocket porn and today's mass-manufactured playing cards are
cheap—in more ways than one—especially the top-shelf variety. But cast aside any
visions of tacky titillation, and feast your eyes on the tasteful and beautifully designed set
of erotic illustrated cards by Lascivious. The independent lingerie company, which is run
by sister and brother team Chloe and Ozzie Hamblen, has employed the services of some
of the best illustration talent around to produce a set of saucy, seductive cards that, while
they might make you blush, do so in rather a sophisticated way.

Playing cards are fairly innocent everyday objects today, but since their
introduction to Europe by Eastern merchants in the late fourteenth century they have had
risqué and mildly subversive associations. Playing cards have not always been as cheap
and disposable as they are today and the Lascivious cards revive the more artful
approach to card design of earlier eras. Before the invention of the printing press and
moveable type in the fifteenth century, playing cards were carefully crafted objects—in
medieval Europe, when the art of the miniature was popular, cards were adorned with
intricate scenes and portraits. Illumination, woodcut and engraving were all used to
decorate cards and they grew in popularity as trade and travel increased, carried from
place to place by merchants who also spread the word about games as they went.
Variations in the visual style of cards grew across Europe as the suit system emerged and
cards have continued to be used as visual chroniclers of the ages, featuring images from
politics, entertainment, sport and popular culture. In eighteenth-century England, when
print culture boomed, playing cards were adorned with the popular satirical cartoons of
the day. In the United States a pack was produced commemorating the American Civil
War—an early example of Americana. The Swiss made a pack celebrating regional
costume in the 1890s. In the 1920s a pack was produced by the Orient-Express, depicting
the train's typical travellers, and was packaged in glamorous fashion, within a satin-lined
leatherette box. There are souvenir cards for almost every subject under the sun.

Under the puritan regime in seventeenth-century England, playing cards were
deemed frivolous and immoral and they have been variously banned and outlawed in
many different ages because of their association with the dubious pleasures of gambling.
Even after the development of printing and the start of mass production, people continued
to produce hand-painted cards as luxury objects. They were the tools of courtly social
rituals—for centuries, card games in fashionable society provided a forum for interaction
between the sexes, flirtation and the acting out of sexual intrigues.

ILOVEDUST
www.ilovedust.com

02

BEN TAN
http://bentan.bellefree.com

01

DED ASS
www.dedass.com

03

04

EMILY ALSTON
www.emilyforgot.co.uk

05

NEWTASTY
www.newtasty.com

06

FIONA WYLIE
www.art-dept.com/illustration/wylie/index.html

© COPYRIGHT HELD BY ARTIST

07

08

BUTTONBROTHEL
www.buttonbrothel.com

FIONA WYLIE
www.art-dept.com/illustration/wylie/index.html

09

BLEACH
mindvomit@gmail.com

10

Chloe Hamblen of Lascivious was inspired to launch her own deck of cards through a long-standing fascination with playing cards and also a love of illustration. While she is responsible for the lingerie design side of Lascivious, her brother, a freelance graphic designer, looks after the rest of the company's visual identity. "Ozzie grew up with graffiti culture," explains Chloe, "and that influenced me and I fell in love with illustration." The process of finding illustrators for the project, she says, was wonderfully easy. "Everyone I asked was really excited to be involved and everyone kept saying 'you should speak to so-and-so' and 'I know someone else who'd be great'— there's a real sense of community with illustrators."

The feeling of collaboration throughout the project was important to the Hamblens and they relished the opportunity to work with illustrators from around the world. The Lascivious deck includes cards designed by, among others, David Foldvari, Fiona Wylie, Kid Acne, Toki Doki, Satoshi Matsuzawa, Jon Burgerman, Richard May and Joel Lardner. The deck comes in a black tin, accompanied by a ribbon-bound booklet introducing each of the artists.

The cards themselves, says Chloe, are "all about play", and the illustrators have produced work ranging from understated to downright raunchy. "I've always found playing cards quite sexual," Hamblen explains. "It's all about power and tension, especially in games like strip poker. And the idea of play ties in perfectly with our ethos, which is all about play and fun in sex."

Despite the undeniably naughty side to Lascivious, the growing business is built on some sound and sensible strategies. It is currently stocked in Coco de Mer and has a slightly more accessible diffusion line in TopShop on Oxford Street, called Lascivious Purple. There are hopes for a larger presence in TopShop, including bespoke wallpaper and mannequins, and there is also expansion afoot in the Coco de Mer camp. The plan— with the help of some interesting projects like the playing cards— is to grow slowly but steadily, and last a long time. Sounds like something else you might find in the bedroom.

14

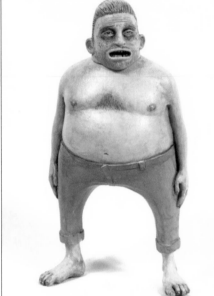

03

05

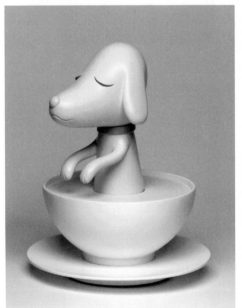

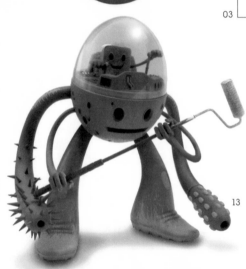

13

07

17

MONSTERISM
island
woodland
volume 3

net.   www.playbeast.com

PLAYBEAST
©2005

12

Best
5 Back Hill, London, EC1R 5EN
+44 (0)20 7833 5544
www.bestshopever.com

Toy Story.

Whatever you collect, there's no thrill quite like getting your hands on that long-coveted latest item to show-off to your fellow fanatics. And if it's toys that ring your bell, look no further than our guide to the all time top twenty, as recommended by Nikki Wadden of Best.

09

[01] <u>KAWS chum in pink</u> (they come in clear, yellow, black as well) I love the shape of this (I love all of KAWS toys), but this is my favourite. Produced by Toygroup 360.

[02] <u>KAWS Companion, glow in the dark version</u> I was too late for this one... sniff.

[03] <u>Tokion v Barry Mc Gee Toy</u> I love the fact you take his head off and there's a mop underneath. Produced by Tokion.

[04] <u>Babapapa toy</u> My all-time favourite character.

[05] <u>Weebles</u> They wobble but they don't fall down... classic. Produced by Hasbro.

[06] <u>Yoshitomo Nara Little Wanderer</u> Beautiful toy, looks like it's made from porcelain, and moves on its wheels too. Produced by Cereal Art.

[07] <u>Yoshitomo Nara Pup Cup</u> Again beautifully produced, spins around of his own accord—amazing. Produced by Cereal Art.

[08] <u>KAWS accomplice, pink version</u> I just love this—but then again—I seem to like all KAWS toys.

[09] <u>Dalek Ice Bots</u> These are a much smaller toy, but again beautifully executed by Kid Robot. I want them all. They come blind packaged, so you never know what you are going to get.

[10] <u>Frank Kozik Giant Smoking Bunny plush</u> Produced by Medicom. I think this is amazing—it's massive and I think that's part of its charm.

[11] <u>Frank Kozik set of flocked Smorkin bunnys</u> Produced by Kid Robot—the pimp version— from one massive version to this much smaller version. I have them next to each other.

[12] <u>PAM Blunt Manana Banana</u> Produced by Kid Robot. I love all that PAM does, they do everything well, clothing, toys, music and pizza.

[13] <u>Jeff Soto Walker</u> This isn't out yet—I can't wait though. Produced by Critterbox. I love Jeff's work, and it's going to be interesting to see his work as a 3D object... I want to get a piece of his art for my kiddies' nursery.

[14] <u>Tattoo Me Keith by James Jarvis</u> I know James has lots of new things, but I love Keith, he's my favourite... produced by Silas and Maria.

[15] <u>Pogeybait by Daniel Clowes</u> He loves donuts, always a plus in my book. Also he's not bothered by carnivorous worms.

[16] <u>Voodoo Doll by Bert</u> I love what Bert does—she always comes up with an interesting twist (see Pumpkin, Mantrap, and Skull toys also), plus these are handmade, so I think that gives them an extra edge. Produced by Bert, www.bertindustries.com.

[17] <u>Big Snorse soft vinyl</u> by Pete Fowler I've just seen this. I love Pete's small Monsterism toys, but it's lovely to see a big version like this.

[18] <u>Dob plush by Murakami, 8"</u> I love all things by Murakami—this plush being all of 8" looks great.

[19] <u>Dehara Oyasai Wars</u> Killer Cabbage and Mini Cabbage from giantrobot.com. Reminds me of the Toxic Avenger.

[20] <u>Grimace</u> Lovely purple fella—I can't think about toys without mentioning him. Enemy of the Hamburgler—given free at Mcdonalds for the last 20 years or more.

06

01

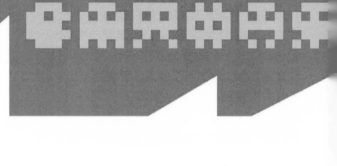

Arcade Fire.

As games become more and more visually sophisticated, striving to re-create reality, there is a growing number of people who are harking back to much simpler times. The 8-bit aesthetic is alive and well, manifesting itself in old school obsessed coders, Space Invader graffiti and even a fashion range by Malcolm McLaren. Here <u>Andrew Losowsky</u> looks at the growing phenomenon that is retro gaming.

02

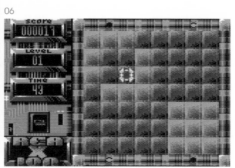

03

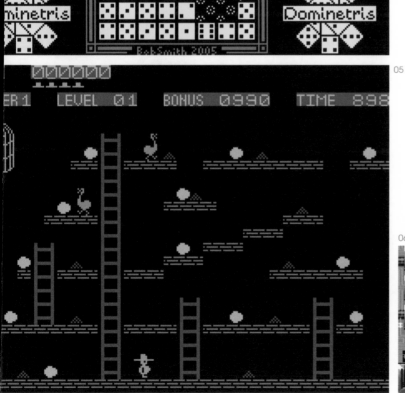

04

05

How fast we've grown. According to those
who count such things, videogame consoles
have now reached their seventh generation
in thirty years. It's a remarkable journey
from Pong to the XBox 360, with technology
repeatedly improving and then fast
becoming obsolete. Meanwhile, other home
tech has remained steady—the VHS recorder,
for example, also came out thirty years ago,
and is only now starting to disappear.

Yet as eBay becomes the elephant's
graveyard of consoles past, many of these
long-forgotten games, along with the
dreaded message "LOADING—PLEASE
WAIT...", live on as an aesthetic, a challenge
and, above all, as something to play. In the
search for ever-more real graphics, have we
really lost our sense of fun?

At first glance, the aesthetic quality of huge,
square-edged pixels backed by simple,
beep-based beats may seem doubtful. There
again, one of the seeming requirements for
retro-chic is that it's slightly naff, and 8-bit is
currently the flavour of choice for a nostalgic
generation. Space Invader graffiti (www.
space-invaders.com) has spread around the
world, designers are building everything
from Pong Clocks to Nintendo Entertainment
System-controller belt buckles. As if to prove
a bandwagon exists, even Malcolm
McLaren has created a range of 8-bit
children's clothing called FASHIONBEAST.

07

06

01 Iam8bit logo for the
     exhibition i am 8-bit 2.006:
     Classic videogames of
     the 80's re-envisioned,
     April 18–May 19, 2006,
     Gallery Nineteen Eighty
     Eight, Los Angeles
02 And I'll Do It Again,
     by Mark Bodnar
     (www.markbodnar.com),
     exhibited at Iam8bit
03 10 Paces,
     by Amanda Visell
     (www.thegirlsproductions.
     com), exhibited at Iam8bit
04 Dominetris by Bob Smith,
     available from
     www.cronosoft.co.uk
05 Chuckie Egg
     screenshot from
     www.chuckie-egg.org
06 Reaxion by Jason Kelk,
     available from
     www.cronosoft.co.uk
07 Malcolm McLaren's
     Fashionbeast 8-Bit
     clothing, available
     from www.yoox.com

01

02

But is it just about fashion and nostalgia? Jon Gibson is founder of the iconic exhibition I Am 8-bit (www.iam8bit.net), where artists and designers create their own reflections on those days when it all seemed so simple. He says, "It's all about love of the old-school—those uncomplicated times when pixels had prowess, before 3D abolished all sense of style. Look at today's fascination with reality—games are judged on their photographic qualities, not their style choices. Too often do you hear a developer pitch their game like this: 'Our models are comprised of 30,000 polygons vs last year's game which only had 15,000.' Lest they forget to focus on the more important aspects of gameplay—storytelling, level design and, most integral, making the game as fun as possible" Even more surprising perhaps than his views is that Jon is just twenty-three years old. "I spent an entire year working my ass off to organise an art show that celebrates an era which I never truly experienced," he admits. "But people are finally recognising that era as something special, something great."

In many ways, the industry has come a long way in thirty years. Videogames are now multi-million-pound ventures embarked upon by licensed studios, and the quality of the graphics is ever closer to reality. A by-product of this has been that the bedroom coder—who once spent hours typing in and then changing the listings from computer-game magazines—has now moved onto internet hacking and file-sharing. Writing games from scratch on a home computer, the beginnings of virtually every senior videogame programmer in the world, just isn't done any more. Pre-Windows, everyone could at least write: 10 PRINT "HELLO WORLD" 20 GOTO 10

But who today types out commands, let alone knows how to do anything without using the mouse? The answer is: small groups of dedicated coders who have retreated to the coalface of the 8-bit obsession. Jason Kelk from oldschool-gaming.com is just one a hardy bunch of codeheads who still write games for, among others, the C64, the Apple II, the Amiga and the ZX Spectrum, trying to squeeze what we've learnt in recent years about gameplay into less space than a typical Word document. Among the attractions for Jason is "the sheer challenge; programming for any 8-bit system is one of those 'you against the machine' situations... Getting something moving can be difficult. Getting a game that looks, sounds and most importantly plays well is a real labour of love."

It's not just about the zen of the task. He describes his games as "pure and simple; no eighty hour-upwards plot arcs with cut scenes". Such simplicity can be powerful. Many feel that the imaginative leaps that basic pixels and text adventures once provided are sorely missing in today's 'show it all' realistic graphics, to which a still-vibrant text adventure scene is testament.

Also disappointed with current gameplay is Roels van Mastbergen, part of Senile Team (www.senileteam.com), which creates "high-quality old-school games, graphics with character and, most importantly, the solid gameplay we feel one can only find in the classic genres". For him, classic videogames outshine current incarnations quite simply because they're less about realism and more about fun. "It's so easy to start playing a classic game. No need to sit through lengthy training levels in order to master the controls, just press start and go. You can figure out what the buttons are for in less than two seconds—quite a difference from many recent games where you have to fight the controls before you can fight the bad guys.

"Another issue is 2D versus 3D. Your screen has only two dimensions. Your D-pad or mouse can only move along two axes. So why try to make games in three dimensions, when you know you can't properly observe or navigate the third one? Because they're more 'real'? Games aren't supposed to be real, they're supposed to be fun. And human brains like two-dimensional thinking. The greatest intellectual games are two-dimensional: chess, checkers, Go... We like to be able to see the whole picture, so that we know when we make the right decisions. But with 3D games, we're always missing part of the picture—sometimes because the character we're controlling is blocking our own view!"

Simple, recognisable aesthetics mixed with the challenge of defunct hardware also led to two of the more iconic music videos of recent times: the Junior Senior music video Move Your Feet by Shynola, created on Amiga Deluxe Paint (downloadable at www.shynola.com/movies/j_s/j_s_download.htm), and the belatedly endorsed Stewdio video for Jed's Other Poem (Beautiful Ground) by Grandaddy, programmed on an Apple II (www.stewdio.org/jed).

And there's a twist in the tale. To a certain kind of twenty-five- to forty-year-old, certain names will still bring out a misty-eyed grin. Chuckie Egg. Elite. Thrust. Defender. Tempest. Manic Miner. These are the rough blocks that our imaginations turned into epic adventures. And many of these best-loved bloop-bleep games are returning.

Occasionally, a licence might spring up with a name from the past, such as the forthcoming return of Sensible Soccer, or the ill-fated Tempest 3000. More often, these games have returned in their original forms, sometimes as unofficial ports to new machines or mobile phones, sometimes via online emulators (try www.classic-retro-games.com/), sometimes as plug-into-your-TV joysticks with games built in, and sometimes also as budget purchases, downloadable for a small fee via services such as GameTap, a company run by the same group and on similar principles as the cable TV channel Turner Classic Movies. "Games such as Yars' Revenge are still really good games," GameTap's Rick Sanchez told Gamasutra.com recently. "It's been re-released half-a-dozen times. It's still fun, it's a good quick hit, and it's something you can play while you're downloading one of our newer games."

Classic games reborn as modern-day 'LOADING—PLEASE WAIT...' screens? Maybe gaming's entered a GOTO loop of its own.

01, 03
    Space Invader street
    art installations,
    Barcelona. Photographed
    by Andrew Losowsky.
02 Me vs. Me by
    Amanda Visell (www.
    thegirlsproductions.com),
    exhibited at Iam8bit
04 Yarron Blues by
    Jason Davis, available
    from www.cronosoft.co.uk
05 Starman vs. Giant Panther
    by Jim Rugg (www.
    streetangelcomics.com),
    exhibited at Iam8bit

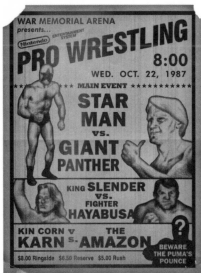

05

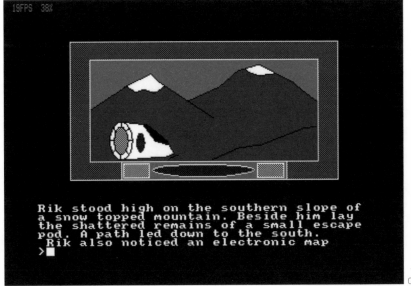

04

Review.

Next Level, Stedelijk Museum, Amsterdam.

Next Level—
Art, Games and Reality
10 March 06 to 18 June 06
Stedelijk Museum CS,
Amsterdam

The Stedelijk Museum in Amsterdam is doing a video-game show. I was kind of excited to hear that it was happening. Apparently it features work by artists and designers who make the vocabulary of games their own, and provide us with their personal reflection on it. So far so good.

I went to the opening and some friends I met outside warned me not to go in there. I told there I had to go in there, I've been asked to write a review of it. Their response? "Oh damn."

It was very crowded but first impressions weren't good. I decided to return in the morning and take my time to give the show my full attention. The next day my suspicions were confirmed: there's no other way to say it, this show is awful.

The show starts with the work of Mexican artist Brody Condon (I think they put him at the beginning because he is from a distant country and he has shown in the Whitney Museum). There is a car-like sculpture, as well as some projections. Condon uses game engines to make animations, which means he takes characters and movements from existing games and makes his own movie. It's a bit like playing a game and moving the character around, like a director instructing an actor and then removing the scenery. One animation shows a God-like figure on fire, the other one is a couple of Elvises dying while floating around.

These works are unoriginal, not pretty, and conceptually boring to boot. Seeing God on fire or Elvis dying just seems very predictable to me, and the fact that they are game characters doesn't make it any better. And besides, icons like God or Elvis have been used so much more effectively in numerous different art pieces.

04

01

02

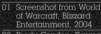

01 Screenshot from World
    of Warcraft, Blizzard
    Entertainment, 2004
02 Brody Condon, Karma
    Physics > Ram Dass, 2005
03 Brody Condon, Need for
    Speed (Cargo Cult), 2005
04 Brody Condon,
    Insurgents (promo), 2005
05 Screenshot from
    Grand Theft Auto:
    San Andreas,
    Rockstar North, 2004
05, 06
    Brody Condon, Karma
    Physics > Elvis, 2004

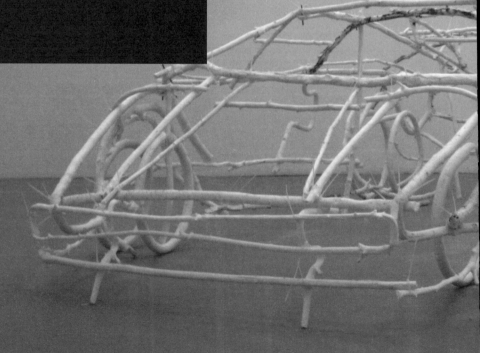

05

06

The rest of the show is even worse. Everything is dark and looks uninspiring. Most of the images have a lot of brown and grey in them. There is a game made by Joes Koppers: people in the exhibition are filmed and projected and when you hit the screen their heads explode. The press release says: "By allowing 'real' people to enter the reality of the game, he mixes our reality with the fiction of the game and demonstrates that the boundaries are becoming increasingly vague." Again, to me this is just extremely predictable—it's just too obvious. You get the point in one millisecond and there is simply nothing else to substantiate it or hold your interest after that. No aesthetic innovation, no poetry, no emotional resonance. Nothing.

The Gamekings also feature in the exhibition. These are a couple of guys who have a cool TV show presenting new developments in the world of video games every week. The show is spontaneous and funny and makes you very curious to find out more. Their contribution to the show is a recording of the pair of them playing GTA San Andreas and World of Warcraft. I understand what they are trying to do— they want to show how awesome these games are, the endless possibilities in interacting with the software and millions of other users simultaneously. To share the sensation of playing a game I think you need to do more than just record it. Watching the games in the museum makes them look really dull, they don't really have any cinematic power when you're not holding the joystick.

This is a missed opportunity for the Stedelijk Museum; it lacks courage. Video games are so groundbreaking and significant in today's digital culture and they have obviously influenced contemporary art.

A historical show would have been far more interesting: an overview of art influenced by video games? Or maybe a showcase of obscure video games? Or of artists who use the language of video games to present surprising ideas and feelings. Why do all the pieces in the show LOOK like video games? There are many artists and designers who take the ideas behind video games and translate them into movies, songs, texts, architecture etc. The curators should have looked further afield and come up with pieces that would surprise visitors to the show. I really wonder why Miltos Manetas has been omitted. He was the first one to bring video games into contemporary art. In 1996 he made movies from video games, video-game performances and prints. These works are poetic, funny, pretty, innovative—in fact, everything I like to see in art. If you want to see a great video-game art piece, check out Manetas's video at www.supermariosleeping.com.

Art, for me, is about intensifying perception. It should be like a friend who stops you for a second and points out something that is worth looking at. Something that was right in front of you for a long time but that you were too busy to notice. When I go to an exhibition, the first thing I want to feel is jealousy: "Damn, why didn't I think of that? That's so beautiful." Or be entertained. I should see something that makes me laugh or cry, or I should learn something. Next Level did none of the above. It made me feel sad, not because of the subject matter, but because it is a miserable show.

Yokoland.

By Yokoland
Published by DGV, £25.99

This offering from DGV is not (as you might be forgiven for thinking) the latest conceptual art-piece from the short Japanese pensioner with the oversized sunglasses—it's actually a book by Norwegian collective (and mates of Kim Hiorthøy) Yokoland. Consisting of Aslak Gurholt Rønsen and Espen Friberg, Yokoland cut its teeth designing record sleeves for a mate's label, Metrononicon Audio, in 2001 and hasn't looked back since. This book shows work to date and makes the reader work hard. There's no quick scanning of the dust jacket to see what it's all about—you have to work through fifteen pages of introduction before you reach the contents page (which is not apparent if, like most people, you pick up a book and then flick from the back to the front). But it's definitely worth the effort as there's plenty of very lovely, very Norwegian work inside. Grafik recommends.

Designing Type.

By Karen Cheng
Published by Laurence King, £19.95

According to the blurb, this book "attempts to bring new depth and insight to the art and process of creating a typeface" and describes itself as being "lavishly illustrated". Unfortunately Grafik found it the equivalent of typographic Mogadon—every time we started reading it we just couldn't help ourselves from racking up the zeds. It's the nearest thing you can get to a typographic textbook. If you are thinking of creating your own typeface and you can bring yourself to fork out nearly twenty notes, then it could be quite a good place to start. There's no doubt that there's some really excellent information lurking within this book's two hundred or so pages, but the experience of reading it is unbelievably dull, and it really shouldn't have to be. Why can't learning about type be fun? That's what Grafik wants to know.

Stencil Graffiti Capital: Melbourne.

By Jake Smallman and Carl Nyman
Published by Mark Batty Publisher, £16.00

Does the world need another book about stencil graffiti? I think we all know the answer to that one. But hey, this one shows the cream of the sten-graf scene from Melbourne, and how many of us have been traipsing around the backstreets of that particular Antipodean cultural hotspot recently? Certainly no one Grafik knows. If this is the sort of thing that gets you hot under the collar and reaching for the spraycans, then you could do much worse than check out this attractive little volume. It's sensitively put together, with an obvious enthusiasm for its subject matter that doesn't come across in that many books. And, as with any self-respecting book on sten-graf, it has its very own section devoted to housewives' favourite Banksy. Ripper.

More Than a Name.

By Melissa Davis and Jonathan Baldwin
Published by AVA, £24.95

Branding—it's something which didn't seem to exist before the 1980s, but which has become essential to anyone who is halfway serious about making their product or service successful in the marketplace now. This book is billed as an introduction to the subject—as with most AVA books, it's jam-packed with nuggets of useful information, well-illustrated case studies and plenty of words of wisdom from a swathe of branding heavyweights. So far, so good, then. But what really lets it down is the design—there's simply way too much going on. Four typefaces (with more than one weight in most circumstances), plus a plethora of coloured and patterned backgrounds, and one particularly annoying background that looks like scrunched-up paper. Maybe they thought that this would appeal to students, but quite frankly it's all over the place. Which begs the question: is AVA truly practising what it preaches with its own branding? Maybe whoever's in charge needs to sit down and read this book.

Review.
Books.

Design It Yourself.

Edited by Ellen Lupton
Published by
Princeton Architectural Press, £10.99

Should we really be encouraging people to 'design it themselves'? Isn't that the problem with so many clients these days? Give them a PC and a copy of Microsoft World and it's bish-bosh, a nice bit of Comic Sans, import some clip art and away you go. Why pay thousands of pounds for a designer? This book seems to be aimed mostly at a teen market ("Not satisfied with the T-shirts on sale at the mall? A CD package for your band?" etc) and was actually written by students from the Maryland Institute College of Art and directed by Ellen Lupton. It's well put together and obviously subscribes to the 'If you can't beat 'em, write 'em a snazzy little design manual' school of thinking. This diminutive little book will, apparently, make the reader "Think like a designer". Hmmmm—is that something that should really be encouraged?

Designing for Small Screens.

By Carola Zwick, Burkhard Schmitz and Kerstin Kühl
Published by AVA, £17.95

This is not a book that would inspire love at first sight across a crowded bookshelf. It's not even the blind date that turns out unexpectedly well. It's not quite the 'if you were the last book on earth' scenario, but it's getting there. Its design can only be described as minging. In fact it makes you realise where the phrase 'left on the shelf' originates from. Which is a shame, because there's some useful content, should you find yourself dipping a foot into the 'user interface' pool of graphic design at any point. It covers everything from mobile phones, PDAs, MP3 players, pockets PCs to games consoles and investigates the challenges involved with designing for these little devices. But it looks horrible. Definitely one to borrow from the college library.

Stickers from the First International Sticker Awards.

Published by DGV, £23.99

A sticker book with sheets of actual stickers—whatever next? Don't get too excited, though, because there are only two little sheets of the little sticky critters. Now that would be much more fun— a grown-up sticker book, like the ones that you had as a kid, only a million times cooler. This book contains approximately 800 entries from the world's first Sticker Awards, which took place in 2005. There's all manner of sticker art here from all across the globe, and the laws of probability mean that there's probably going to be something that takes your fancy. There's one thing that Grafik wants to know, though. Forgive us for verging on the existential, but what's the point of doing a book on sticker art and then just showing the artwork? Surely a sticker's life only really starts when it's been peeled back and slapped on a lamppost?

At the Edge of Art.

By Joline Blais and Jon Ippolito
Published by Thames and Hudson, £19.95

A neat little book which examines the new breed of art—that's art that's created for cyberspace rather than the traditional gallery environment. Split into sections including Code As Muse, Preserving Artificial Life and Redefining Art, it's bursting with interesting projects that challenge the traditional notions of art, often lying somewhere between conceptual art, science and information design. The works shown here are so much more than digital doodlings—they are varied, often intriguing and often very complex projects that deserve to be investigated further. An excellent book, in Grafik's humble opinion.

Review by Rob Hinchcliffe

Published by DGV
Price £9.99
www.die-gestalten.de

Review.

Vortigern's Machine and the Great Sage of Wisdom.

By James Jarvis and
Russell Waterman

It's all Star Wars' fault.

Before George Lucas came along with his merchandising masterplan, the words 'action figure' didn't mean that much to the youth of the Western world. But when Darth Vader et al made the leap from 'just a toy' to 'precious collectable' they instigated a seismic shift in the psyche of millions of (mainly) little boys the world over.

Up until quite recently the action-figure industry hadn't shifted much from its conception in a galaxy far far away. Then, in the late Nineties, along came an artist by the name of Michael Lau who accidentally kicked off the 'urban vinyl' movement in Hong Kong when he created an original action figure in order to photograph it for a record cover.

At around the same time in London, a Japanese friend of illustrator James Jarvis suggested that he should think about turning the simplistic, child-like drawings he'd been sketching since he was a kid into a plastic moulded figure for the fashion company Silas. As a result Jarvis's most famous character, Martin, was born and the cult of James Jarvis was spawned.

Born in London in 1970, the young Jarvis found himself captivated by the likes of Richard Scarry, Hergé and Dr Seuss. This fascination continued until he was able to learn his trade studying illustration at the University of Brighton and then at the Royal College of Art.

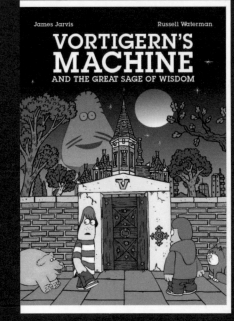

As a result Jarvis has always maintained that he is first and foremost an illustrator, creating fantastical characters and entire worlds for them to inhabit on paper before converting them into three-dimensional figurines for grown-up Star Wars kids to spend their grown-up pocket money on. Now, with the publication of Vortigern's Machine and the Great Sage of Wisdom (written with Silas founder Russell Waterman), Jarvis has finally been able to pen a narrative for his creations, inverting the old 'story first, action figure second' model in the process.

The narrative of Vortigern's Machine, as you might expect, is not too complex. Jarvis's heroes are two twelve-year-old boys named Rufus 'Rusty' Ethelred and William Ignatius Guthrum (Wiggs to his friends). On a trip to the park, Rusty's clinically obese dog, Dworkin, accidentally ingests Wiggs's door keys and the pair have to find a way of getting them back.

As plots go it's not exactly The Lord of the Rings, but as the story progresses through oversized monsters, drug-induced visions, intrepid explorers and of course the Great Sage of Wisdom himself, Tolkien undoubtedly springs to mind, as do The Wizard of Oz and Monty Python's Flying Circus.

This is a typically British tale of eccentricity brought up-to-date with pop-culture references and Jarvis's own brand of daffy, naff punnery (at one point Wiggs goes to try on a helmet belonging to the Victorian explorer Lemuel Waverly and is inevitably reprimanded for "taking the pith"). It's all amiable enough stuff but it's difficult to shake the feeling that the words are there simply to give the illustrations a reason to exist. But, then again, how many of this book's target audience will be buying Vortigern's Machine for its narrative stylings?

Jarvis's illustrations are undoubtedly the book's main attraction and, thanks to the fact that all these characters began life as pen-and-ink sketches, the conversion from 3D action figures to 2D cartoon panels is seamless.

Despite the fact that Jarvis's main characters are nothing more than a collection of simplistic geometrical shapes he manages to extract a fantastic range of emotions out of their bulging, spherical eyeballs and paper-cut mouths (noses don't exist in Wiggs and Rusty's world, it seems) and each member of the extended cast sports a brilliantly detailed, often hilarious, costume (a throwback perhaps to the inherent demands of the action-figure industry).

If any criticism can be made about Vortigern's Machine's stylistic quirks it's that at times the whole thing looks a little sterile. It's obvious that Jarvis loves to draw but it also seems that the computer plays a large part in his work. For example, almost every page in this book contains at least a few panels in which the background has been rendered using fairly crude colour gradients and the overall effect can be quite ugly when it's placed right next to Jarvis's otherwise simple and effective style. We know that toy collectors like to keep things nice and clean in their boxes but maybe it would have been nice if James had allowed himself to colour outside the lines every now and again.

Having said that, it's quite obvious that long-term James Jarvis fans are going to love this book simply because his name is on the front cover. They'll cheer every time another familiar character makes an appearance and they may even buy two copies so they can leave one unopened. Whether it will find an audience outside the fan club remains to be seen.

01

Play—it's anything that we do when we're not working and resting.
To coincide with this month's Special Report, we asked some of our favourite image libraries for their interpretation of the word 'play', and here are the results.

Play Date.

02

03

National Portrait Gallery.

Tom Morgan.
Head of Rights and Reproductions.

You can see Honey Salvadori's fantastic picture of Adam and Joe as an icon of play, an allegory of the connection between a very British sort of playfulness and creativity—at first it seems chaotic, until you notice the structure which holds it together.

Christie's Images.

Mark Lynch.
Marketing and Development.

Substitute the traditional marionette for the latest movie tie-in action figure and this early sixteenth-century Chinese illustration shows how little has changed.

Alvey & Towers.

Emma Rowen.
Picture Library Manager

Play relates not only to childhood but throughout our lives. As we grow bigger so also do our toys. Play means many things to many people. Maybe these boys played together as children; now we see them playing in the traditional sense and also 'playing' their music.

04

05

Corbis UK.

Georgina Spiller.
Communications Specialist.

This iconic image of the Playboy trademark by Warhol evokes a world of hedonism and pleasure. An innocent bunny came to represent so much more than cute, but who was doing the playing and who was getting played? The girls serving drinks in exclusive clubs were constrained in tight costumes and high heels and were treated as frivolous objects to boot, but for the majority of girls they were having the time of their lives. Liberated from dull jobs, they earned great money and socialised with the elite. Of course there's a fine line between empowerment and having a good time but there's no getting away from a great logo is there?

Image Source.

Gianni Brancazio.
Marketing Executive.

Play is the order you get as a kid from your mum when you're under her feet and getting in the way: "Go outside and play"—it's not punishment; it's an excuse to round up your gang and head out to play in the park. This image shows that it's never too late to head back to that park.

The Bridgeman Art Library.

Ed Douglas-Home.
Marketing Executive.

Handball Players by Max Ferguson, one of the 500 contemporary artists represented by Bridgeman, shows a typical Brooklyn sporting scene in the artist's home city. It displays the artist's remarkable skill in photorealism—without close inspection this appears to be the work of a photographer, not a painter.

06

Mary Evans
Picture Library.

<u>Lucy Talavera.</u>
Senior Account Manager.

This is a great picture. I love the strong shapes and bold contrasts which give the image such a strong sense of movement. It represents play with great simplicity; as something innocent and free, long before anyone had heard of a PlayStation.

PunchStock and
UpperCut Images.

<u>Tim Hook.</u>
Sales and Marketing Director.

This image reflects children's natural tendency toward role-playing games. Role-playing, make-believe and fantasy transcend technology, and ultimately the idea of entering new worlds and perspectives has been the basis for some of the most popular video games—think Zelda, The Sims, and even prior to that, Dungeons and Dragons.

Getty Images.

<u>Rebecca Swift.</u>
Director, Creative Research.

Play is something that adults don't do enough of. As a result we see adults messing around and acting like children in advertising. It is something we wish we had more time for because it combats stress, gets those endorphins racing and reminds us what it was like to have no cares.

01

02

03

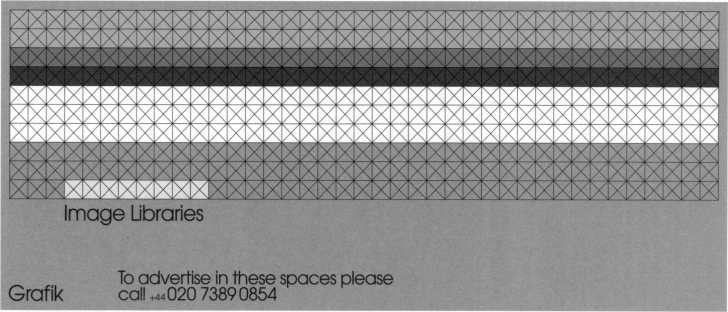

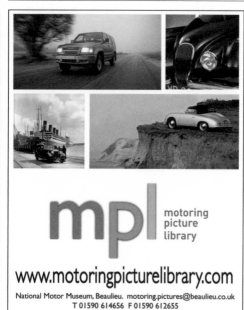

Progress are market leaders in the production of creative packaging. To reserve a copy of our new special edition brochure, contact us now.

Call +44.(0)1484.608.600
sales@progresspkg.co.uk
www.progresspkg.co.uk

highly finished packaging mock-ups

for examples please visit our website
www.finish-creative.com
or contact lee robinson
phone : +44(0)20 7251 2122
lee@finish-creative.com

finish

< PACK   MOCK-UPS >

37-42 compton street london ec1v oap

foil blocking

www.istprintin
gservices.co.uk
e. info@
+44 (0)1655
331196

Creative
Creative Resources
Resources

To advertise here
please call
+44 020 7389 0854

Grafik

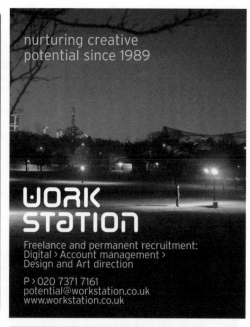

WE LOVE MAGAZINES COLOPHON 2007

BIZART.LU

BRAND MANAGERS - CREATIVES - PUBLISHERS - STUDENTS

>INTERNATIONAL MAGAZINE MEETING
>EXHIBITIONS, TALKS, PARTIES
>WORLDWIDE ONLINE DIRECTORY OF POP CULTURE STYLE MAGAZINES

colophon

09-11.03.2007 LUXEMBOURG
www.colophon2007.com

COLOPHON 2007 IS PRODUCED BY MIKE KOEDINGER
IN COLLABORATION WITH CASINO LUXEMBOURG - FORUM D'ART CONTEMPORAIN
WITHIN THE FRAMEWORK OF "LUXEMBOURG AND GREATER REGION EUROPEAN CAPITAL OF CULTURE 2007"

VICTOR|BUCK

We'd love to hear from you—send us
your typographic work, ideas and events to
typo.grafik@gmail.com

Alphabetti Spaghetti.

Lucille Tenazas and Neville Brody take centre
stage in Bologna for Graphic Design Day 02—
it actually last for three days (it runs 6–8 April)
and is based in two locations in the city, with
the usual mix of exhibitions, conferences and
debates. There's also a chance to see the
FontFont exhibition FiFFteen if you haven't
done so already. Contact Valentina Spina at
v.spina@graphicdesignday.info for details.

Girls on Type.

This month the St Bride Library celebrates women
in printing and the graphic arts by way of an
exhibition that runs until 27 April. Entitled The
Distaff Side and curated by printing historian Paul
W. Nash, the show looks at the role of women as
printers from the fifteenth century to the present
day. The exhibition is open Tuesday–Thursday,
12.30–5pm (9pm on Wednesday). For further
details, go to www.stbride.org

Ten-Year Itch.

Doesn't time fly—it's ten whole years since
Rian Hughes unleashed Device Fonts onto an
unsuspecting world and here's a lovely little
volume to celebrate the fact. There's an intro
by Erik Spiekermann, words of wisdom from
Mr Device himself, plus acres and acres of
Device fonts in all their multifaceted glory.
The book is published in softback and available
now from www.type.co.uk—but one lucky
Grafik reader can win a copy of the extremely
limited edition of 150 signed and numbered
hardback copies. To enter, simply email
giveaway.grafik@gmail.com and tell us what
your favourite device is.

This Month in Typo__Grafik:

The poster shown reads:

Vrij 27 jan 06
Open
10.00-20.00
dag
Gerrit
Rietveld
Academie

Gerrit Rietveld Academie
Fred. Roeskestraat 96
1076 ED Amsterdam
tel. 020 571 16 00
www.rietveldacademie.nl
bus 15, bus 170
sneltram 80, tram 16

HBO-opleiding Beeldende
Kunst & Vormgeving,
Vooropleiding en
Oriëntatiecursus

Class Act.

We know that some of you look down your finely
kerned typographic noses at it, but we love
Avant Garde here at Grafik, and it's always good
to see an inventive use of one of our favourite
fonts. This rather lovely poster was created for an
open day to attract new students at the Gerrit
Rietveld Academy in Amsterdam by two very
talented fourth-year graphic design students,
Ingeborg Scheffers and Marrielle Frederiks. The
students (who were commissioned by visiting
lecturer Linda van Deursen) started by applying
a range of patterns onto each letter.

In order to take this idea further, they chose two
different weights (book and bold) for each letter
and placed them on top of each other to create
new letterforms. These were then adjusted to fit
the posters, map and signage within the
building. The letters are randomly scaled and
this, combined with a bright colour palette, gives
off a playful impression—perfect for enticing
those wet-behind-the-ears potential students.

i_scheffers@hotmail.com
marrielle@zonnet.nl

Typo__
Showcase.

Rust Bucket.

As a rule, here at Grafik we try to avoid featuring designers' own identities (because if you can't get your own identity right, then you might as well give up), but we've made an exception to the rule for this particular one. The identity in question began life as an experimental project called Random Words in Random Places by designer Toby Tinsley. The project itself is pretty self-explanatory, except that the random words (which are created in designers' favourite Helvetica Bold) are made up from letters that are a foot high and are hewn from solid steel. The letters were welded onto four-foot-high posts and the steel was left untreated.

They were then placed in various random locations and left to rust, with striking results. Tinsley liked the project so much he decided to use the resulting imagery to form the identity for his new design agency, which he named rather aptly Twentysix Letters. Tinsley will continue to shoot the letters throughout the year, both in urban and rural locations—if you happen to be touring the Highlands this month, keep a look out for some four-and-a-half-foot-high steel letters gently rusting in the freezing forty-five-degree Scottish rain.

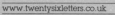

www.twentysixletters.co.uk

FF Meta Book It

ABCDEFGHIJKLI

ghijklm

6789

Anatomy of a Typeface.

FF Meta

Love it or hate it, there's no denying Meta's might as a typeface. The font Erik Speikermann developed for the German Post Office later boomed into a sprawling type family that has been known to get the most rigorous typographer's knickers in a twist. Here, Yves Peters discovers how Speikermann went about designing the font and guides us through the labyrinth of its later lives.

When we see the expansive superfamily that FF Meta has become, it's hard to believe its beginnings were so humble. As its designer Erik Spiekermann explains, it was first developed for the German Post Office in 1985 as PT55. "I wanted to create a modern text face that was as legible as a serif and as clear as a sans without being neutral and boring. The client had originally not asked for an exclusive typeface, but it had become apparent that none of the existing faces at the time could solve all the problems a corporate font for such a large enterprise faces (no pun intended)."

Spiekermann's approach began with an analysis of existing fonts—twenty in total, from Helvetica and New Gothic to Syntax— to determine which properties would work and which wouldn't for his new face and the context in which it would be used. "A geometric sans wouldn't have been legible enough at very small sizes and on bad paper, and a serif was not acceptable for cultural reasons. So I gave the letters little pseudo-serifs, which also opened the potential ink-traps between down-strokes and curves. These little swerves guide the eye along the top of the x-height, where most differentiation occurs."

The way Meta was developed gave it characteristics quite distinct from its predecessors. "Meta has more contrast than Helvetica and other 'neutral' sans faces," says Spiekermann. "The counter shapes are squarish, while the outlines are round. The contrast between those two shapes creates a little tension and makes letters more discernible. In continuous setting, all those details (counter-contrast, pseudo-serifs, cut-ins) become almost invisible, but add warmth. In faces like Helvetica, outside and inside are pretty much concentric forms, giving not enough distinction and making most letters look like each other."

FF Meta Book ▶

ABCDEFGHIJKL

abcdefghijklm

0123456789

!@£€$™%^*

©® LF ITAl

HIJKLM

HIJKLMNC

0123456789

FF Meta Bold Roman
ABCDEFGHIJKLMNOPQRSTUVWXYZ
abcdefghijklmnopqrstuvwxyz
0123456789
!@£Đ$™%^*()_-—
+={}[];:''""",.?/~<>
©®

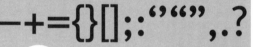

FF META BOLD ITALIC CAPS
ABCDEFGHIJKLMNOPQRSTUVWXYZ
ABCDEFGHIJKLMNOPQRSTUVWXYZ
0123456789
!@£€$™%^*()_-—+={}[];:''"",.?/~<>
©®

FF Meta has developed into one of the great FontFont families of contemporary sans serifs, with eight weights (from Hairline to Black), a condensed version and special character sets for Cyrillic, Greek, Turkish, Baltic and Central European languages. Today it is FontShop's bestselling type family.

The Meta family has known three different incarnations, and thus there tends to be some confusion about which version is which. So let's clear the air and explore the history of the most successful humanist sans of the previous decade, 'the Helvetica of the Nineties'.

Originally, back in 1991 when the second batch of FontFonts was released, there was FF Meta (Normal, Bold, Small Caps). One of the defining characteristics of FF Meta—and FontFonts in general—was the presence of hanging (or old-style) figures and additional ff-ligatures in the 'regular' Normal and Bold weights, while lining figures were found in the Small Caps weight. The distinctive Meta arrow occupied the slots for the lesser-than and greater-than symbols. The first expansion came in 1992 with FF Meta 2, adding three more weights (Italic, Italic Small Caps, Bold Small Caps).

FF MetaPlus, released in 1993, was the big leap forward. It introduced three new weights—which effectively tripled the number of fonts to eighteen—and included a fine-tuning of some characters (most notably a correction of the crossbar on the lowercase 't') and revisions of spacing and kerning. The family at that point featured Normal, Book, Medium, Bold and Black weights, all in Roman, Italic, Small Caps and Italic Small Caps (except for the Black weight, which didn't include Small Caps). Still hanging figures in the 'regular' weights and lining figures in the Small Caps. The latter featured the Meta arrow, while lesser-than and greater-than symbols were added to the 'regular' fonts.

Eventually, in 1998, it was back to FF Meta. This saw a reorganisation of the family into subfamilies: FF Meta Normal, FF Meta Book, FF Meta Medium, FF Meta Bold and FF Meta Black, all in Roman, Italic, Small Caps and Italic Small Caps, which all got coupled with their respective Expert and Lining Figures weights: yep, a whopping sixty fonts. Biggest change this time was the addition of the Black Small Caps, and moving of the extra ligatures (ff, ffi, ffl which were previously in the 'regular' fonts) to the new Expert fonts. And the lining figures' weights meant that you don't have to switch between 'regular' fonts and Small Caps fonts any more to get the desired type of numerals. Of course, the story doesn't end there: the latest—and definitive—incarnation of FF Meta got subsequently expanded with foreign-language versions, a Condensed family, additional light weights (Light, Hairline and Thin) and just recently a group of Headline cuts.

So, to conclude—never mix the original six-weight FF Meta with FF MetaPlus or the new FF Meta family, as it has different spacing and kerning, and some redesigned characters. Substituting FF Meta for FF MetaPlus is recommended, but keep in mind that ff-ligatures will disappear and types of numerals might differ.

Corey Holms
www.coreyholms.com

A delicate, expressive face revived by a master of reduction? A conservative typeface harbouring a very naughty letter? Corey Holms unravels the tantilising mysteries of <u>Linotype Didot's Italic</u> lowercase 'v'.

V for Victory. V for Vendetta. V for Linotype Didot Italic... the original Didot letterforms were created by Firmin Didot for the family publishing business in France at the turn of the nineteenth century. This marked the beginning of modern typefaces; Giambattista Bodoni was simultaneously at work. Modern type is exemplified by a lack of bracketed serifs and either horizontal or vertical lines being pushed to an extreme level of width or attenuated form.

The Didot publishing house typeface became a popular stepping-off point for new revival faces in the early 1990s. HTF Didot and LP Didot were created by Jonathan Hoefler and Garrett Boge at roughly the same time. This resurgence of older typefaces was spurred on by the ability of the designer to digitally reproduce the delicacy of forms that had previously been relegated to professional typehouses.

At this point you're probably wondering why this particular cut of Didot italic looks so different from the other versions currently available. It's because it was revived in 1991 by Adrian Frutiger, better known for his more geometric modernist typefaces, such as Univers and Frutiger. Who would have thought that someone whose beliefs were that letterforms should be reduced to their simplest essence would choose to re-create such an expressive/exuberant typeface?

Frutiger was highly influenced by the interplay between white and black and the visual balancing of the two. While some typefaces seem either optically very heavy or very light, even in its bold weight Linotype Didot retains a harmonious relationship between the positive and negative shapes in the letterforms. The original Didot typeface is one which bridges the gap between the traditional and the contemporary, and Frutiger builds on that strength.

Although the roman and uppercase italic of Frutiger's version conform to the Didot standard, the lowercase italic is where the true character of this cut is revealed. This group exudes a sensuality and humanity not seen in the almost sterile roman and uppercase italic forms, nor does it appear in either of the other two cuts of the period.

The lowercase 'v' is the perfect example of the naughtiness hidden inside the externally staid Didot family. While the roman letterforms are a type of outerwear that the whole world sees, the lowercase 'v' is the Agent Provocateur undergarment that thrills the chosen few. It is bold, confident and sexual. It teases the designer into wanting to use it every time a 'v' is required. It lets the world know that there is room for playfulness and fun within the rigours of strict modernity. It's the dark horse of the type world.

V for two fingers to the rest of the modern typefaces...

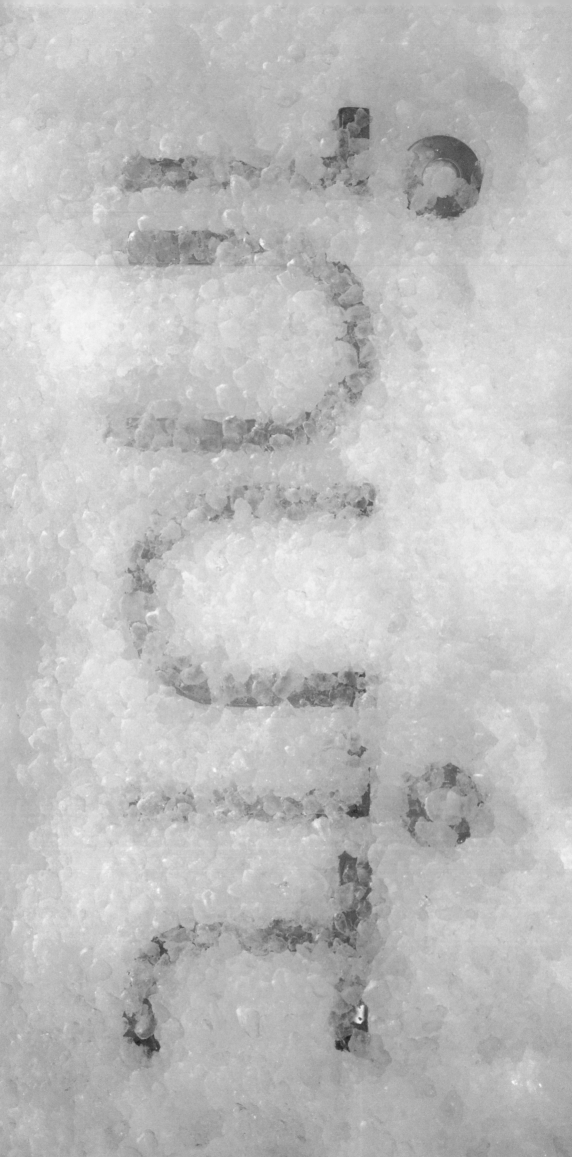

Issue N°2
Objekts of Desire.

Welcome to the second instalment of Objekts of Desire, where we seek out the most **delectable new design goodies for you to win**. This month we have toy designers extraordinaires Friends With You's lovingly hand-crafted Malfis and an exclusive collection of works by man-of-the-moment Zak Kyes. So, feast your eyes, fire up your brains, answer the questions and get them in to **giveaway.grafik@gmail.com** by 30 April. Bonne chance.

Friends with You.

With all that sun and vice, Miami must be a fun place to live, so it's no surprise that it is the home of Friends With You. These designers and toy-makers have the kind of overactive imaginations that we heartily approve of. Their world is a self-made phantasmagoria of warped invention and curious creatures. The latest addition to the splendid Friends With You family is the Malfis, mischievous wizards intent on mayhem. The unutterably enchanting trio of plush toys, courtesy of the generous chaps at Friends With You, can be yours to cuddle and play with at will. Just tell us the name of the Malfi who sports spots. If luck doesn't smile upon you, don't worry—there are plenty of friends to admire and buy on the Friends With You website.

Zak Kyes.

London's Kemistry Gallery is one of the precious few spaces dedicated to graphic designers' work. Since its inaugural show in November 2004, it has staged some excellent exhibitions on individuals including Geoff McFetridge, Parra and the Cut-Up collective. In March this year it had another hit with All That Is Solid Melts Into Air, a show of work by super-talented Zak Kyes, which became an instant must-see. Mr Kyes and the Kemistry people have kindly come up with a special Zak Kyes collection especially for Grafik readers to win. It consists of two limited-edition signed posters, a T-shirt, a badge and the invite and envelope from the show. How's about that, then?—some future design classics for your collection. To be in with a chance, just tell us in which city Kyes currently resides.

Friends With You
www.friendswithyou.com
Zak Kyes Group
www.zak.to
Kemistry Gallery
www.kemistrygallery.co.uk

Next Issue **Grafik**   N° / 140

Special Report
<u>Information Design</u>

What's your secret ambition?

Tom Evans.

Mook
www.mook.com

My secret ambition is to go back to school.
No, not in order to drink milk and play cops
and robbers but to teach. I have this fantasy
of myself as a slightly older chap, swanning
around an art college wearing a trilby, or
maybe something more sinister—like a cape.
I'd mumble profound things and inspire people
in an off-hand but friendly way. I'd be loved
by many, disliked by a few but respected by
all. And I'd have a moustache. No, a ponytail.
A really long (waist-length) grey ponytail.
Students would approach me sheepishly in the
bar and ask my advice about kerning, antique
websites and Adobe Flash™ CS IV. They'd nudge
each other as I told quaint stories about 'print'
and showed them yellowing copies of Grafik
from before it became a video Podcast. Granted,
some of the students would fancy me but only
the really attractive ones and I would never
abuse my position of responsibility, would I?

Hector Pottie.

MadeThought
www.madethought.com

My secret ambition is to be able to play a
musical instrument. Specifically the fiddle.
To be able to play it to a level that I can just
pick it up and play and it sounds beautiful.
I wasn't interested in playing music as a child
but now really wish I had been and applied
myself. It's not something that is likely to
happen soon. Finding time for anything new is
difficult and there are many other things that
need my attention right now. But it's a nice
thought that maybe when I'm eighty I'll be
able to play a few tuneful notes.

Tom Muller.

Muller/Kleber
www.hellomuller.com/www.kleber.net

Secret ambitions that were just too
impractical: become an astronaut, a superhero,
a Jedi Knight.

Secret ambitions that looked realistic,
but then I got sidetracked: become an
Egyptologist, a comic-book artist, a superhero.

Secret ambitions that I actually achieved:
leaving Belgium and building a good career in
design abroad, working at agencies I respect,
finding my own 'artistic voice', and getting
involved with comics.

Secret ambitions still on my list: design and write
a sci-fi novel/comic, a monograph on my Dad's
work, graphic and conceptual design for film,
design more for comics, develop a pop-culture
brand/icon.

Secret ambitions that actually look realistic at this
point in time: design more for comics, design and
write a sci-fi novel/comic. Become a superhero.

Joe Burrin.

Spin
www.spin.co.uk

01.
Climb more mountains. I need to escape
flatland every once in a while.

02.
Print more fabric. Sometimes the digital world of
graphics makes me feel such a Luddite and the
product can be so ephemeral. Fabric has a life
beyond just being itself—you can turn it into a
tea towel, some curtains, or even a cushion
cover (lovely).

03.
To turn a pastime into a trade. I have a
propensity to collect and hoard bits and bobs;
there's no rhyme or reason, it's just stuff I like. I'd
love to open an Eye-Candy Emporium—a place
of reference and inspiration for anyone
interested—Snooper's Paradise meets the Pitt
Rivers Museum meets the Francisco Capelo
Collection with a healthy dose of Charity Shop.
I like the idea that someone might take away
something that will add to their lives; it would
also give me a continued excuse to keep
finding and buying.

Frith Kerr.

Kerr | Noble
www.kerrnoble.com

When I was young I always wanted to be
Jennifer Hart from Hart to Hart. A few fashion
disasters, bad hairstyles, unsolved cases and
years later I still haven't given up. I still want to
look good while solving crime—only now it
involves having a guest spot on CSI.

Grafik Magazine
Third Floor, 104 Great Portland Street
London W1W 6PE

Phone +44 (0)20 7637 5900
Email hello.grafik@gmail.com
www.grafikmagazine.co.uk

Publisher
Alan Lewis

Editor
Caroline Roberts

Deputy Editor
Angharad Lewis

Sub-Editor
Robert Shore

Editorial Intern
Fravashi Aga

Design
Nick Tweedie
Yasuko Ikeda

Marketing Manager
Madelaine Bennett
+44 (0)20 7637 5900

Circulation Manager
Adam Long
+44 (0)7961 007139

Sales Executive
Tim Kantoch

Sales Executive
Michelle Fairlamb

Editorial Contributors
Jonathan Bell writes about architecture for Wallpaper* and is co-editor of things magazine. Laura Clayton is a Leeds-based freelance writer. Corey Holms lives in Southern California and is an art director at entertainment design agency Mojo. Angharad Lewis is deputy editor of Grafik. Andrew Losowsky is a Madrid-based writer. Caroline Roberts is editor of Grafik. Erik Spiekermann is an all-round type guru and a frequent flyer.

Special Thanks this month to Yasuko Ikeda.

Grafik is supported by

Wace Corporate Print
www.wace.co.uk

Fonts
ITC Avant Garde, ITC Lubalin Graph
Supplied by yellowblack.com

Paper
Grafik is printed on Inuit—
a new paper by Arjowiggins
www.arjowigginsfinepapers.co.uk

Grafik is published by Grafik Ltd.
Grafik ISSN No. 1479-7534

Grafik Subscriptions
Subscriptions line +44 (0)870 428 7957
Email grafik@cisubs.co.uk
or subscribe online at:
www.grafikmagazine.co.uk

Advertising Sales
Orange 20
20 Orange Street, London WC2H 7EF
Phone¹ +44 (0)20 7321 0701
Phone² +44 (0)1372 802 800
Fax +44 (0)1372 723 322
Email sales@o20.co.uk

Advertising Production
DFP Design
+44 (0)1306 888 458
adsart@dfpdesign.co.uk